Fear in the Long House

(*formerly* The House that was Afraid)

Jenny Bray

Scripture Union

130 City Road, London EC1V 2NJ

This is the combined and abridged edition of two books
'Longhouse of Fear' and 'Longhouse of Faith', previously
published by the Borneo Evangelical Mission.

© Borneo Evangelical Mission
First published in this form 1974
Re-issued as FEAR IN THE LONGHOUSE 1978
Reprinted 1978
Reprinted 1982
ISBN 0 85421 584 0

Printed and Bound in Great Britain by
Purnell and Sons (Book Production) Ltd., Paulton, Bristol

Fear
in the
Long House

1

As he stepped out on the long-house verandah, Ding entered a hive of industry. All down one side the women stood on the narrow platforms against the wall, pounding the husked rice, while their small children staggered and crawled around them.

The men sat on the platforms that ran along the outer side of the verandah, splicing rope, carving paddles and sharpening parangs.

Lihan was sitting at the far end where it was quieter. Ding made his way to him and sat down.

After a while, Lihan looked around them and then, in a low whisper, said to Ding: "Have you heard there is to be a 'pakat aban'?"

"No, when?" Ding questioned half eagerly, half apprehensively.

"In a few more days, I think," Lihan informed him. "The old men say it is the season for one."

"What's a 'pakat aban'?"

They looked up quickly. Little Imang had sidled up in time to eavesdrop. He hated being out of things, and Ding and Lihan were always plotting and planning together. Seeing Lihan's cautious look had made him even more curious than usual, though, had he but known it, Lihan had not been conscious of people wanting to eavesdrop, but rather of the evil spirits and their mysterious power. "Go away and play, Imang." Ding spoke rather abruptly.

"I want . . ." began Imang, but the look in Ding's eyes warned him that he had best retire gracefully, lest a more undignified exit be forced upon him. He went off grumbling to himself, more curious than ever. It was unlike his brother Ding to be so secretive.

Ding watched him go. He was sorry he could not explain

it to the little fellow, but he was not yet old enough to have the responsibility of such knowledge. He would probably get it all mixed up and the secret would be out in no time. "Pakat aban" meant a fishing spree with the use of juice from the tuba vine, but one hardly even dared to think of it. There might be something that could read one's thoughts and inform the Balira fish.

The Balira fish were said to be the witch-doctors of the river. Legend has it that, years ago, the fishes became troubled because they had no witch-doctors and no fish wanted to be one. Finally, the Balira fish consented to be a witch-doctor on one condition: Every fish must give it one of its bones. They all agreed, with the result that the Balira fish then became so full of bones, that no one wanted to eat it.

The Balira fish increased in numbers and, as witch-doctors, they became very powerful. They had friends in the jungle, too.

It was for this reason that the Kayans had to be so careful and give a code name to this particular kind of fishing, in which the whole village took part. If the beetles, bats or birds heard that a day of tuba fishing was afoot, they would tell the leaves of the trees, who would in turn tell the Balira fish. The Balira fish would then work a charm that would bring abundant rain and swell all the streams suitable for tuba fishing, and spoil all the plans of the village. The old men of the village could tell many a tale of tuba fishing plans ruined by someone's indiscretion.

"It's a long time since we had a 'pakat aban'," reflected Ding thoughtfully.

A nudge from Lihan brought Ding out of his reverie. "Look who's coming!" Ding looked, and saw a boy of about their own age coming toward them. His sullen features, swaggering walk and supercilious air marked him as an unpleasant character, which indeed he was, and no one thought so more than Ding.

He hated Anyi almost as much as Anyi hated him. In

Anyi's case it was a matter of jealousy: Ding had always been popular with old and young alike. The latter looked on him as their leader, a position which Anyi coveted and tried to gain by constantly reminding everyone in general that his father was the most powerful witch-doctor in the village. He bullied and bossed the younger children, and mocked and taunted those of his own age. He knew that none dare touch him lest some evil be brought upon them by the witch-doctor.

Anyi stopped in front of the boys and, ignoring their obvious displeasure, sat down with them.

"Catch a lot of fish this morning?" he asked in a leering fashion, which suggested he already knew the answer.

"Few only," replied Lihan as courteously as he could. He knew better than to leave the talking to Ding on this occasion. "The red hawk flew over," he added briefly, in the hope that Anyi would be satisfied with that and go on his way. It was a vain hope.

Anyi was bent on irritating Ding. "Ah, the red hawk," murmured the boy. "I wonder what evil is going to befall you."

The boys did not reply.

"You are silent this morning, Ding," Anyi went on. "Has fear taken hold of your tongue?"

Ding ignored the question. "I have better things to do," he said curtly.

"Ah! Always so polite, the noble Ding." Anyi paused and smiled as though something amused him very much. "I, too, have work to do. Sit well, you two," he added, as he rose to go.

"Go well," returned Lihan, more from habit than goodwill. Ding did not even look up.

"I don't like his words. They were bad, I think," muttered Lihan. "He is going to do something bad."

"You speak truly," said Ding. "But there will come a day when his bad words will return to him and harm him. I would like to see it."

2

"You will soon see for yourself," Ding laughed down at his young brother. The whole village was agog with preparation for the "pakat aban", and Imang was thoroughly exasperated by the mystery of it all.

He and the other younger children had been questioning their elders for the last three days. "It's a meeting with the monkeys in the jungle." "It's riding down the rapids on a crocodile." "It's collecting beetles to train for pig hunting." These were some of the infuriating answers they received. Infuriating, not because they did not believe such things could happen, but because, by the very variety of the answers, they realised they were none the wiser.

Lihan came into the room, paddle in hand. "Did Taman Lehei say we could have his canoe, Ding?"

"Yes," replied Ding. "I put a sprig of tree in the prow, so everyone will know it is reserved."

"I'll go and tell the others then," said Lihan, "there will be eight of us, I think."

The river bank was a scene of gay confusion. Canoes, varying in length from ten feet to eighty feet, bumped side by side in the river. Men, the more dashing of them dressed in bright red loincloths, leapt from canoe to canoe and from canoe to river bank, waving their parangs fiercely, though harmlessly. Some collected branches and saplings from nearby, and made long curling shavings to decorate the canoes.

In contrast to the men, the women wore short, black skirts, though these too were edged with borders of red. It was in the wearing of beads that women excelled. Masses of large, dull-coloured beads of varying hues—heirlooms passed down through the ages—hung round their necks

4

like so much tangled vine around tropical trees. Imang was heard to ask in tones of awe, "What would happen if one of those women fell into the water?"

The young children, dressed mainly in bare-skin, frolicked, dived and swam. The big day had come and, whatever a "pakat aban" was, it was going to be exciting.

Ding and Lihan, having collected six of their friends, made their way through the noisy, busy crowd, laughing and talking as they went.

Their borrowed canoe was at the end of the row, and they did not realise until they were almost into it, that it was occupied.

"Anyi!" exclaimed Ding.

There he sat, gazing up at them insolently. In his hands was the twig which spelt "reserved" to any Kayan.

"Ah! There you are, my friends," he said, sneeringly. "I have been waiting for you. This thirty footer should do us well." His meaning was unmistakable. He, Anyi, was their self-appointed leader, and they were to be his obedient crew.

Swallowing his mounting anger, Ding said stiffly: "We already have a crew for this canoe."

"Oh, hello, Ding. I didn't notice you there." The condescension with which Anyi acknowledged Ding's presence was extremely irritating. Anyi was out to make the best of a situation which gave him one of those rare opportunities to humiliate Ding before his friends. Nor was he unmindful of the collection of girls who were standing by giggling.

"A crew!" Anyi sounded puzzled. "Yes, you can be one of the crew, Ding." His tone implied that he had no further time to listen to childish prattlings. "You have your tuba vine, I see." Anyi then started issuing orders with domineering bluster.

There was nothing else to do but to obey.

Ding was given a place of little importance in the canoe.

Anyi himself took the all-important position of leader and guide in the prow.

It was just as well for the safety of them all that Anyi, for all his cowardice and bluster, was, regarding river travel, a true Kayan. He possessed all the nerve, skill and daring that the hazardous riding of the Akah River rapids required. Knowing this, his crew, while despising him for his contemptible behaviour, were ready to obey him to a man in the rapids. So much depended on quick, decisive thinking on the part of the leader and obedience on the part of the crew.

All the way down the rapids, the canoes raced and jostled with one another. Men, women and children whooped and shouted. Even Ding forgot the anger rankling in his heart as they fought their way through rapid after rapid.

Through gorges of towering, moss-covered cliffs, past mountains of green foliaged splendour they went, coming at last to the tributary where the tuba fishing was to be held. Going up-stream was necessarily slower. But with great enthusiasm, they poled in the shallows and paddled in the deep, until they reached the fishing place, some two miles up-stream.

Soon the river bank was alive with the rhythmic pounding of the tuba vine. Some of the small canoes were half filled with water, and, as it was pounded, the sticky white fluid from the vine was washed into them.

Some of the people had stopped further down-river, and were putting the finishing touches to a wall of twigs and leaves with which they dammed the stream.

One of the older men stepped forward. He beckoned two men to follow him into a small canoe in which there was a very small amount of tuba. Pushing off up-stream, they poled along till they came to a small pool formed amongst the rocks. Here they tipped in the white milky fluid while the old man chanted:

"O spirit of the rocks! Of the wood! Of the flat stones! Of the rapids! Of the earth and of the leaves! Here in this pool is your share of the numberless fish. Spoil not our sport by any interference."

The other small canoes of tuba fluid were now taken to the middle of the river and overturned. Slowly the fluid began to spread through the water. The same old man went ahead of all the others and, as the first fish rose to the surface, he speared it. Throwing it on to the shore, he shouted to the spirits that here was a fish for them and they were not to begrudge the few that he and his tribe would catch. This final offering to the spirits having been made, the tuba fishing began in earnest.

As the tuba penetrated into the depths of the river, fish of all sizes rose to the surface, suffocated by the poisonous fluid. Scoop-nets waved, spears flashed, canoes hustled and pushed together. Men, women and children scooped, speared, laughed and shouted. Several times it seemed that Imang would have his desire in seeing what would happen if some heavily beaded woman fell into the water. Not that Imang was likely to notice at that stage, as, armed with a small three-pronged spear which Ding had made for the occasion, he was entirely engrossed in using it. The object of his spearing was the fish, but it was only due to the skill of those nearest him in getting out of his way that he did not spear something bigger in his excitement!

Ding, his troubles forgotten for the time, sought to spear mainly the large, rare and much coveted Tabi fish. So successful was he, that his catch was noted by the long-house chief who commended him for his quickness and skill. The chief's praise was balm to Ding's wounded pride of the morning, especially as he saw the envious look on Anyi's face.

As the afternoon wore on, the dam was reached. Here there were literally hundreds of fish. Some, not quite overcome by the tuba, leapt the dam: others slid through cracks that were appearing in several places. Some of the canoes went on downstream to catch the strays, and others returned upstream. A few stayed where they were, spearing and scooping at their leisure. As night fell, fires started to appear along the river bank, and the work of smoking and cooking the fish began.

It was a very happy and satisfied people who ate till they could eat no more, then sat or lay around the campfires talking of the day's doings. The older men began to tell tales of the past head-hunting days before the white man took over their country and abolished such pleasures from their way of life.

A tired but very happy Imang struggled unsuccessfully to stay awake and listen to the tales being told. Finally, falling asleep on the stones, he dreamed of fish, bigger than Tabi fish, which he bravely captured with a large scoop-net and trained to accompany him on head-hunting forays.

It was in the early hours of the morning that Ding fell asleep and he too dreamed of fishing and head-hunting. But in his dream every fish had the name of "Anyi", and every head he collected was Anyi's head. He wasn't finished with Anyi!

3

A FEW days later Ding and his father made their way toward the sprinkling of small rice huts at the back of the long-house.

When they reached their hut, which was built about eight feet above the ground, on wooden piles, Ding picked up the notched log which lay underneath. Placing it in position, he climbed up. He untied the jungle vine which held the little door in place, and crawled in, followed by his father.

Inside, it was dirty, dingy and dark. Ding's father looked at the tall woven baskets piled in no particular order in the little room. "Only two baskets remain," he remarked ruefully, indicating two baskets standing upright in the corner.

"Two baskets of rice, and we haven't started to plant yet. How are we to live?" There was a mixture of fear and bitterness in Ding's voice.

His father shrugged. "Who knows?" was his only answer as they set to work to replace the leaves of the roof which had rotted and decayed.

"When are we to begin our farms?" Ding asked after a long pause.

"They are to choose the hawk man tonight," replied his father.

Ding looked startled. "That means the omen hunting begins tomorrow?" he questioned, though the answer was obvious.

"Yes, and we should begin farming in another fifteen to twenty days."

"Any idea who will be hawk man?" asked Ding, as they

made their way to the river for a bath.

"No, the committee men don't know themselves yet. I don't think it has been discussed."

It was almost dark when Ding and his father returned to the house. Ding's mother informed them, as she gave them their evening meal, that they were about to eat the last of the fish from their tuba fishing trip of several days ago. This news was received in gloomy silence. It was not a good time for fishing, wild pigs were scarce, and it was obvious by the little that the women folk had been able to collect of late, that the vegetable fern tips were also scarce.

The only one of the family who was unaffected by the announcement was Imang. He was carrying his evening meal around in his grubby little fists and eating as he played.

The meal over, Ding emerged from the tilung to find a few girls had gathered on the platform waiting for his sister Mujan. He whiled away a few minutes in teasing them, which was obviously appreciated by all, except one girl who ignored him, pretending interest in the band of coloured beads around her wrist.

Usun Imang was an attractive girl with a quick, bright manner and sparkling brown eyes.

Almost from the day of her birth, there had been an arrangement between her parents and Ding's that the two should marry. They were now at an age considered suitable and, although nothing had been said, both knew that their parents were preparing to discuss the matter and arrange the wedding.

Leaving the girls, Ding wandered through the rooms to Lihan's room. He always ignored Usun with the same intensity with which she ignored him. Nevertheless, that didn't stop him thinking about her at times and wondering whether she liked him. Not that it mattered . . . if their parents said they were to marry, marry they must.

Lihan was preparing to leave as Ding arrived. "I was

about to come to your room," he said. "The girls are in our room," Ding told him as he sat down on the platform.

Other boys drifted in and they all crowded together on the platform. Ding strummed on a guitar-shaped, three-stringed instrument.

"Is your canoe finished?" The speaker was a pale-faced youth, who was covered from head to foot with a scaly skin disease, which was prevalent amongst the tribe.

"Yes," said Ding and Lihan together. "And not a crack in it," went on Ding.

"Did you hear that Anyi's canoe split in two places when he was burning it?" asked another of the boys.

Ding and Lihan exchanged a glance of malicious pleasure. "I didn't know," said Ding. "He would be angry, I think."

"He was very angry," returned the boy, and they all laughed. No sympathy was wasted on Anyi.

There was a slight disturbance as a man came through the little door from the next room.

"Planning a head-hunting trip, are you, boys?" he laughed, and went on his way without waiting for a reply.

"Is there a committee meeting?" asked one of the boys.

Ding nodded. "They are going to choose the hawk man tonight."

"Thank goodness I'm too young to be hawk man," said Lihan.

"We'll be old enough in time," sighed Ding.

The hawk man was chosen each year. He was the omen seeker of the people for the beginning of the farming year.

For fifteen days or more he must live on a platform off the verandah, specially built for the occasion. He could not lie down during the day, could not speak to anyone, and must eat only dry rice and salt.

"I wonder what would happen if we didn't have a hawk man!" mused the scaly youth.

They all looked at him aghast. "No hawk man!"

exclaimed Ding. "It's bad enough when we do have one!"

There was a general murmur of agreement. "Even though we have the hawk man and obey all the omens from one harvest to the next, we never have enough food."

Ding grunted discontentedly. "All that work, and we get enough rice for three or four moons, and starve for the rest."

Everyone looked apprehensively around. The feeble flame of the tree-gum lamp flickered and fluttered, sending grotesque little shadows skipping about them.

Ding shivered—he had been more outspoken than was wise. Suppose the spirit had heard him! Lihan broke the uneasy silence: "Remember that white trader who visited here and was so drunk they had to tie him to a post until he was sober?" he asked of no one in particular.

The boys laughed. "Who could forget him?" exclaimed one boy. "That was the first time I had ever seen a white man . . . and the last time," he added thoughtfully.

"What about him, Lihan?" asked Ding.

"I was thinking about him saying we ought to follow his God."

"Did he say that?" asked one of the group.

"Yes; my father told me. He said that the white man wasn't afraid of evil spirits and just laughed at our omens. He said if we followed his God we wouldn't be frightened either."

"My father said that all white men follow the same God and call themselves Christians," put in the scaly youth.

"And they really aren't afraid of the spirits?"

"No. This white man told Anyi's father to call any old spirit he liked; he wasn't scared."

"What did Anyi's father do?"

"He didn't do anything. He said later that if anything happened to the white man the government would send soldiers to kill us, like they did when our grandfathers wouldn't stop headhunting."

"We ought to have found out more about his God."

"The chief tried to, but the white man only spoke the language of the Malay people and being drunk, he spoke it so badly that no one could understand him."

"It's a pity we couldn't have found out a bit more."

"Oh, I don't know. The chief asked him if he would take one of our men down to Long Nit in his canoe. At first he said 'yes', then suddenly changed his mind. He said it would make thirteen in the canoe, and that was an unlucky number."

"Unlucky number! Well, what's the difference between that and our omens?"

"That's what the chief said. He decided we might as well stick to the omens we know, rather than learn a whole lot of new ones. Also he said the white man's God can't be a good God because the white man was a bad man. If He was a good God, good men would surely come and tell us."

"Yes, and who knows whether our spirits might be stronger than his God and then we would be in great trouble."

Ding put down his instrument and stretched himself out on the platform. "There is no way out, I think," he yawned despondently.

The other boys also lay down to sleep. It was their habit to sleep together in whatever room they happened to be.

It was not until the following morning that Ding discovered his father had been chosen as hawk man.

4

THE following days at Long Nangah were filled with fearful foreboding. No one seemed to know why they were afraid, yet everyone was.

With much reluctance, Ding's father took on his duties as a hawk man. From now until the omen-seeking days were over, no one dare mention his name. He would be referred to as "the hawk man".

It took a lot of persuading to convince Imang that he could neither visit his father as he sat on his crude platform built off the verandah, nor speak to him from a distance.

On the first day that the hawk man was installed, a number of people gathered at the back of the long-house. With their parangs, they cut a track through the jungle for about half a mile from the long-house. Here a post was erected with a little shelter attached.

After the people had returned to the house, the hawk man set out to begin his first brief vigil. This visit to the jungle was the only time that he was allowed to leave his platform.

Ding felt he could have almost gathered up handfuls of fear in those first three days. It seemed to seep through the house like a thick mist.

These first three days were the most important, as so much depended on the sighting of the red hawk by the hawk man. During this time the people were forbidden to leave the long-house.

On this occasion the hawk man saw the hawk two days running. This was made known to the people by the smoky fire which he lit immediately after he saw it. The smoke also informed the hawk that the people were expecting it to bless their crops.

The fact that the hawk man did not see it on the third day was disappointing, as it would have meant the promise of a good crop. However, everyone felt conforted that at least the crop promised to be fair.

On the fourth day, everyone was allowed out of the long-house to look for fern tips and collect wood. Pig hunting and fishing were forbidden.

Following this day of comparative freedom, the hawk man's search for the rain bird began, after which came the search for the barking deer, then the hornbill, and finally the civet cat.

Each search was supposed to take three days. It had always puzzled Ding that in the brief time the hawk man spent at the place made for him in the jungle, he saw all these omens in their correct order.

Sometimes the omen-seeking took longer than the three days allotted. They seemed to be particularly elusive for Ding's father, and his lonely vigil went on and on.

The older men grumbled that it was because a younger man than usual had been chosen. "Such a man would not have the wisdom of his elders," they reasoned.

Ding didn't understand what they meant, until he heard a whisper that in the case of the latter four omens, the hawk man was at liberty to pretend that he saw them. This bewildered Ding more than ever.

When, after twenty-six days, the omen-seeking came to an end, Ding was tempted to ask his father if he had really seen any omens at all. However, his father, thin and gaunt from his long vigil, was in no mood to be questioned. For a week, he seemed despondent. Nor did the large quantities of rice beer he consumed during that week help to improve his temper.

As far as his family was concerned, he was not really restored to the family circle until Lihan's father spoke rather forcibly to him about his responsibilities. After that, he roused himself from the depths of his drunken despair and went to help with the farm.

The omen-seeking over, the people were now at liberty to make their farms. The families of Ding and Lihan shared a farm. This year they had been allotted a large piece of virgin jungle on a steep mountain side. Both families went to their land in the early morning, and came home just as the sun was setting. Others, whose farms were too far away, lived in temporary shacks built on their land. As each phase of the farming year ended, they returned to the long-house.

Imang found himself left each day in the charge of Lihan's young sister. Poyang was a thin, worried girl of about ten years of age. She found Imang and her own little brother almost more than she could manage. Imang hated being left at the long-house—it was so lonely. There were just a few very old people there and a few very young.

On their farms, men and women worked hard and long cutting down the undergrowth. Then the heavier work of felling the trees began. As this was the work of men, the women were free to give all their attention to cooking rice and looking for fern tips.

Imang was very happy when the felling of the trees began, for it meant he could go to the farm and spend the day with his mother and Mujan.

When they were half-way through the gruelling task felling the trees, Lihan's father saw a red-headed snake. His gasp of dismay caused the others to turn around and they saw it too. They all stood transfixed! It was not the beauty of its flaming red head and tail, in contrast to the black and light blue markings of its skin, that attracted them; it was the message of its presence that kept them standing there in horror-stricken silence.

Finally they turned away, their faces suddenly weary, their shoulders sagging. They must leave this land and look for another place to build a farm. The red-headed snake had warned them.

The next piece of land was another mountainside of virgin forest. Desperately, they worked to get the land ready for burning. The burning off was not a success. Because they were late preparing the land, they missed the spell of dry weather and had to burn off while the wood was wet. That meant the added burden of gathering the half-burnt branches and undergrowth into little heaps, and trying to burn them further. It meant that the soil did not benefit from the burning off—it meant late planting and, most heartbreaking of all, backbreaking toil with little return. A poor crop was inevitable.

When the planting season was over, the long-house resumed its usual busy life. Ding and Lihan worked on their canoe, but somehow the joy had gone out of the work. They felt tired and depressed. It was not that they were unaccustomed to this atmosphere of subjection to the spirits, the omens and witch-doctors, it was the growing realisation that there was no escape. There must always be this struggle for existence, the fear of disaster, and at the end—but they didn't dare to think of the end.

Adding to their general depression was the realisation that their supply of rice was almost finished. Soon they would have to eat the thick, tasteless sago which never seemed to satisfy. The thought of it gave them a choking feeling.

Coming in one morning from a fruitless attempt at fishing, Ding threw the net to the floor and flung himself on to the platform.

He was about to pour out his own troubles, when the door of the next room suddenly opened and a little ball of energy rushed past them into the tilung.

There came a low pleading murmur from within, followed by the sound of movement, and a triumphant Imang emerged.

Two long black and white feathers waved frantically from a plaited band of spliced jungle vine, which threatened to fall over his eyes. In one hand he half carried, half dragged a black wooden shield. In the other was a piece of wood shaped like a parang.

Ding raised his eyebrows comically. "Where to?" he enquired.

"Head-hunting!" was the brief and bloodthirsty reply, as the little lad vanished from sight.

"Another skull for the verandah," smiled Mujan.

"I hope it's not Imang's," grinned Ding.

Judging by the noise he was making when he came bursting in again a few minutes later, Imang still had his head, but it was not a very happy one.

"What's the matter, O Head-hunter?" asked Ding, taking the tearful would-be warrior on to his lap.

"Anyi," gasped out Imang between sobs, "took my cap."

Ding frowned, "Anyi who?"

"Anyi La'ing. Hit him, Ding!"

As Ding's grip tightened on the boy, a surge of anger swept over him. What other Anyi would it be? As if all the other things were not enough, but you had to put up with types like Anyi as well.

"Hit him, Ding. Get my cap back."

Ding stared at the lad looking up at him so trustfully. There was no doubt in Imang's mind that his brother was a match for the bullying Anyi.

"Where is he?"

"Out there!" Imang's chin pointed toward the verandah.

"Be careful, Ding," Mujan said anxiously as Ding suddenly dumped Imang on the floor and made for the verandah.

Anyi was half leaning, half sitting on the verandah rail, the cap in his hand. He was obviously not expecting

Ding and looked up in some surprise as he saw him bearing down upon him. His surprise gave way to a malicious smile as Ding came up to him and his hand tightened on the cap.

It was Ding's intention to grab the cap from Anyi and disappear. He snatched at it, but Anyi's grip was firm. "Careful, careful," he said tantalisingly. "Such manners!" It was too much for Ding. All the pent-up feelings of the last weeks found vent in the push that he gave Anyi.

With a cry of fear Anyi fell backwards over the verandah rail. Leaning over, Ding could not help laughing as he looked at him. Anyi was obviously unhurt, but he had fallen into a pig wallow. He rose spluttering and spitting, covered from head to feet in black slimy mud. Beside him two irate pigs, disturbed from their muddy sleep, snorted indignantly.

People rushed to the verandah rail to see what had happened. They burst into peals of laughter which became more hilarious, as pig after pig rushed up and stood grunting and snorting at the luckless Anyi. Imang, who had rushed out to see what his brother was going to do, laughed louder and longer than anyone else. For days Anyi was to be irritated by a chubby, cheeky little figure pointing at him and going off into peals of exaggerated laughter.

For the present, an enraged Anyi, conscious of the laughter of his fellows and in particular of Imang and Ding, slunk off to the river. Trailing after him were half a dozen pigs, still trying to work out what it was all about!

Ding turned back to his room. He was still laughing, but almost unconsciously a sense of fear began to cloud his victory. Anyi wouldn't let him get away with that!

5

It seemed to Ding that this was a bad dream he was reliving. There was Anyi lolling back in Taman Lahei's canoe, the same arrogant expression on his face, and twiddling—could it be the same piece of twig?

There also stood the giggling females, all ears and eyes.

Once again the boys looked helplessly at Ding. This time there were more of them. They really expected something of Ding, too. The news of his brush with Anyi had spread, and he was now a hero.

"Some of you boys will have to find another canoe," Anyi commanded.

"You can come in with me, Ding." His tone suggested that Ding needed someone to see he held his paddle properly. There was also an undertone of warning in his voice.

Outwardly Ding was calm, his face expressionless, but his thoughts were in a turmoil.

He had had a bitter-sweet taste of freedom from fear in pushing Anyi off the verandah rail. Now he faced the choice of humiliation, or of taking a step which, it seemed to his fear-ridden mind, must mean the death of his whole family.

At this point he was unexpectedly rescued from his dilemma by the chief. Today was one of the days that the village gave to working on the chief's farm.

The chief, about to leave for his farm down-river and seeing the boys gathered together, strolled over to them. Oblivious to the explosive atmosphere, he smiled at them.

"Huh, Ding," he said, addressing the boy he knew to be

their natural leader. "You're splitting this group up and planning to give us some thrills in canoe racing, eh?"

Later, Ding and his companions were to recall with much laughter the absurdity of the chief's remark. However, for the moment, Ding could only smile weakly and wonder what on earth to say. He was saved the effort of replying by the chief's further remark: "There is another thirty foot canoe over there," pointing with his chin in the direction of a canoe half hidden in the bushes. "It is heaver than Taman Lahei's, but no doubt you can handle it."

Had the chief chanced to glance at Anyi during his conversation with Ding, he would have wondered at his peculiar colouring.

Ding's smile broadened happily. "We have only one canoe," he said. "We will get that one straight away." The chief nodded. "We'll expect to see some real racing from you boys," he said, and went on his way.

Ding did not give Anyi a backward glance as he made off, together with the other boys, to get the chief's canoe.

A fuming Anyi found himself the sole possessor of the once coveted canoe, a fact which did not cool his anger.

In the end, Ding had to send half of the boys back to Anyi, for he could hardly be expected to man the canoe alone, and the chief was expecting a race.

Anyi and his crew were well on their way when Ding and his company pulled out, a fact of which both crews disapproved. Ding's canoe was already handicapped by being heavier. However, Anyi was out to win the race by fair means or foul.

"Ho! Paddle!" cried Ding as he and his crew flew after their opponents.

The first four rapids were negotiated with ease, and the boys whooped down them joyously. The next rapid, situated on a bend, was one to be treated with a great deal of caution. However, Ding was in no mood to be cautious. Standing tensed on the prow of the canoe, he surveyed the approaching rapid. Then he flung out an arm to indicate the direction to be taken. In the stern, Lihan as steersman gave his paddle a deft twist almost simultaneously with Ding's direction. In a matter of seconds, they were flying headlong down the rapid.

The waves crashed in upon them. "Lever! Lever!" Ding's voice was almost lost in the roar of the water. Levering, twisting, turning their paddles, they guided the canoe through the rapid. They kept it from being drawn into the full force of the waves, eddies, and whirlpools, while avoiding the prominent jagged rocks all about them.

They reached the bottom of the rapid, wet and panting, but with the light of battle in their eyes.

"Ho! Paddle!" they cried in unison as, with a bloodcurdling yell they careered on through the rapids, taking hair-raising risks, determined to pass their opponents. Between rapids, two of the boys bailed furiously so that the boat should not sink.

Great was the excitement when, emerging from a cascade of flying spray, they sighted Anyi's canoe not far ahead. They paddled even faster so that the next strip of calm water found them racing side by side.

For both crews it was an exhilarating race to be won; for their leaders it was an opportunity to defeat the enemy, and these latter two did not join in the general fun. Their eyes were on the approaching rapid, the most notorious of all and the last one before the chief's farm.

Both knew that there was only one channel considered safe for use through this rapid. Only one of them could go down at a time—one would have to fall back. It became obvious to Ding that he would not be able to pass Anyi before reaching the rapid, and that Anyi's canoe was more directly in the course of the channel than his.

He thought of the chief probably watching to see who

would win, and of Anyi's triumphant sneer. Suddenly a bold plan flashed into his mind. There was another channel through the rapid, but by reason of its narrow entrance between two jagged rocks opening into a cauldron of turbulent water, it was never used.

Standing poised on the canoe prow, Ding gave the signal. If the boys had any doubts as to Ding's wisdom, they gave no sign of it, their paddling did not falter.

Next minute they were hurtling through the opening and were picked up by strong waves and hurled down the rapid. They fought frantically yet skilfully for control of the canoe, half standing, half sitting, now certain to capsize, now on an even keel.

There was a moment of comparative calm when Ding took in two vital facts: They were now in shallow but forceful water, and were being swept on to the cliff on the bend. With a shout, he leapt out of the boat, followed as one man by his crew. In a matter of seconds, they had pointed the canoe to the right and leapt back into the canoe with split-second timing. Down they swept into the tossing waves and round the bend, missing the cliff by inches.

They arrived at the foot of the rapid, gasping, spluttering and triumphant. They were ahead of the others and swept down the strip of calm water with flashing smiles and sparkling eyes.

The chief and some of the tribe, who had witnessed the boys' reckless action, reprimanded them loudly as they clambered out of the canoe. Their reprimands, however, were without a sting. Reckless and foolhardy they knew the boys had been, but they were heroes just the same, and the story of their thrilling race was talked about for days.

Anyi's crew were as loud in their praise as anyone, but Anyi himself was surly and sullen. He had been fairly beaten, but it would have been out of character for him to take it graciously.

As the young people worked that day, the race was the

main topic of conversation, and Ding came in for no small share of praise.

Ding was not averse to all this praise. To be truthful, he enjoyed it and was particularly pleased to note that Usun Mangi kept very near to his sister Mujan, who, of course, was not far from her brother.

As for Imang, Ding carved him a small canoe, and with this Imang could be seen demonstrating from morning till night to anyone who would listen, his brother's epic ride through the rapids.

He particularly delighted in showing it to Anyi, who pretended to ignore him. But Anyi was already planning his revenge.

6

DING groaned. His head felt as though someone was beating it with a paddle. He opened his eyes—then shut them quickly. Even the dim light of the room sent darts of pain through his eyes into his throbbing head.

"Ding, I'm hungry!"

Ding gritted his teeth and opened his eyes again. Imang was sitting beside him, pounding on his chest with two grubby little fists. Ding caught hold of his arm. "Stop that and go away," he ordered harshly, and closed his eyes again.

Imang looked at him. Ding never spoke to him like that. It made him feel frightened and insecure. He whispered to himself and looked uneasily around the room. Lihan and two other boys were spread out on the platform. Lying huddled on the rubbish-strewn floor, three more boys slept restlessly, muttering unintelligibly.

From the tilung came loud, irregular snores. Imang whimpered a little louder. He had tried waking first his mother, then his father, and now Ding. None of them would wake up and give him something to eat. Mujan? Where was Mujan?

"All right Imang, stop snivelling, I will help you." Ding's voice, though not kind, lacked its previous harshness. Imang stopped whimpering and looked hopeful.

Ding sat up clutching his head as though it was going to fall off. "I also," sympathised Imang. "What makes our heads sick, Ding?"

"Beer," muttered Ding as he staggered over to the little door-window which opened on to the "backyard".

As he threw it open, he recoiled from the strong sunlight which streamed in. "Must be afternoon," he said half to himself.

"Yes, and I'm hungry," came the plaintive cry. Things were moving too slowly for the emptiness in Imang's stomach. Ding was about to answer him angrily, then checked himself. Poor little fellow—it wasn't his fault.

He tried to think. Somewhere in his befuddled mind there was something unpleasant. What was it? "Curse Anyi," he thought. "If he hadn't made me drink all that beer, I wouldn't be feeling like this." How Anyi had known he didn't like drinking was more than he could say. He always drank a little; he didn't dare refuse it. Every man, woman and child drank. Anyone who refused a drink was held down and the beer was forced down his throat. Ding had always managed to get by with a small amount, but this time Anyi had hardly left him. For the three days and nights of the feast Anyi had stood over him refilling his cup.

"Ding, wake mother up!"

"Be quiet for a minute and let me think, Imang."

Ding's mind went back somewhat clumsily to the arrival of the headman from down-river. He had come to discuss the marriage of his daughter with the son of the chief. Some weeks previously, everyone had been ordered to make rice beer in preparation for his coming. For most people it had meant using the last of their rice, for no one could bear the shame of not having beer for a feast. The feasting had started on the evening of the arrival of the headman and his party, and had continued for three days and nights.

Ding ran a hand through his hair and tugged at the strip hanging down his back. That early part of the first evening had been all right. He had managed to drink very little. It wasn't that he didn't like beer; it was what it did to people that made him loathe it. His usually calm and sensible mother became a simpering idiot, and the serene and gracious Mujan a giggling fool. As for his father . . . his temper was unbearable.

"And I'm just like him," thought Ding.

The woeful little lad suddenly became the centre of his attention as he was violently sick. "Beer makes me sick," gasped Imang. "That horrid woman made me drink lots."

And then Ding remembered! That woman! That was it!

"Ding, she said she'd take me home. I don't like her — she's got awful ears." Imang's hunger and sickness were forgotten for the moment as he recalled how the woman had petted him and make him drink beer all the time. He hadn't liked her, but when he tried to run away she always caught him again. Everyone had been too drunk to notice.

Ding's groan was almost a sob. That woman, Anyi's sister, had married a man from down-river and had gone to live at his long-house some four years ago. Ding heard that she had no children and was looking for one to adopt. Never in his wildest dreams had he thought of her adopting Imang.

It was Anyi's suggestion, of course. This was what he had been waiting for—the arrival of his sister. He must have known she would come in the headman's party. This was to be Anyi's revenge—or as Anyi had said at the feast, the beginning of his revenge.

Ding clenched his fists. They wouldn't get Imang. His parents wouldn't allow it. Four of their children had died before Imang arrived and he was the apple of their eyes. What if they were too scared to refuse? Ding pushed that thought from his mind. After all, Anyi's family were only very distantly related. It was quite common for childless relations to ask for one of the children of their kin, but it was not as if Imang was one of a big family. Of course, it could not happen. They could appeal to the chief if the demand was too persistent; but could they?—or would they?

He thought of Anyi's sister. She did have horrible ears. They had not stretched into nice thin loops like most Kayan girls' ears. The flesh was all lumpy and knotty. Most of all, Ding hated her cunning eyes and scornful smile—so like Anyi himself. Let her adopt Imang? He'd rather see the little boy dead!

A long sad sigh reminded him that the little boy in question was very much alive and with him at the moment. "All right, little brother, I'll see what I can do about getting you something to eat."

Imang brightened. That sounded more like his big brother. Ding rose slowly and painfully to his feet. He couldn't imagine what was holding his head on. Surely it was going to fall off? He staggered over to the tilung. "Is Mujan in here?" he asked Imang.

"No, don't know where she is."

"Wait here then, and I'll see if I can find her," said Ding, as he stumbled into the next room and so on from to room, looking for his sister. The long-house, always dirty and untidy at the best of times, was in a state of filthy disorder. People sprawled in all directions. Here and there a baby or child cried or yelled in a vain attempt to waken its drink-sodden parents.

Ding found Mujan in Usun's room. The two girls were lying in a drunken sleep on the platform. Ding kicked the dishevelled Mujan several times with his foot. It had no effect. He might as well have kicked a log. Leaning down, he shook her and tried to drag her to her feet. Mujan opened unseeing eyes, grunted, and closed them again. In disgust, Ding let her slide to the floor. Going over to the corner, he took up a bamboo of water and emptied it over her.

This had the desired effect of bringing her to a sitting position, and before she knew what was happening to her, she was being hustled through the rooms.

When they reached their room, Mujan was still dazed

and uncomprehending. Ding pushed her toward the tilung. "Imang's hungry. Cook him something," he ordered.

"Mujan, I'm real hungry," emphasised Imang, taking her by the hand and looking up with big, pleading brown eyes.

"Hungry," said Mujan stupidly. Ding gave her another push.

"Light the fire and cook some sago," he commanded, irritated by her slowness.

Mujan moved forward and all but fell into the tilung. Ding heard her fumbling, and after a few minutes, a tiny flame of fire could be seen. He sat down on the platform and leaned wearily against the wall. Beside him, Lihan gave a loud snore and rolled over. He started to sit up, thought better of it, lay back and went into a sound sleep once more.

"Ding, that nasty woman isn't going to take me away, is she?" "No," said Ding determinedly. "No, she is not."

Imang sighed contentedly. With that load off his mind, all he had to worry about now was food, and Mujan was getting that ready. Life had not yet become complicated for Imang. True, he was aware of the ever-present fear pervading the long-house. He was aware of the rule of the spirits and was mortally afraid of them. The various omens and their meanings puzzled him. The witch-doctors filled him with awe. However, he felt secure in the knowledge that his family were always on hand to comfort and help him, and these other things as yet caused him little concern. He could not, at this stage, be expected to see the cruel hand of fear and custom as it stretched out toward him. Nor could he understand why Ding suddenly hugged him so hard that he couldn't breathe, and muttered: "It can't happen. It can't happen."

7

It was late afternoon when Ding joined Lihan. The boys sat on the verandah and leaned on the rails. Ding, brooding over the thought of Anyi's sister and Imang, did not notice that Lihan was unusually quiet and thoughtful.

Suddenly Lihan nudged Ding with his elbow and pointed with his chin. Following his gaze Ding saw a young girl feeding some pigs. Her back was to them, but he recognised her as a friend of Mujan's. He raised his eyebrows enquiringly at Lihan.

"My parents have chosen that girl for a wife for me," said Lihan.

"A wife!" exclaimed Ding. "Isn't that rather sudden?"

"Apparently they have been thinking of it for a while," replied Lihan. "I know my mother hasn't been well and she has been saying she needs a girl to help her with the woman's work. But I didn't know she was thinking of a wife for me."

"Too bad. If your sister Poyang were a little older it would be all right," sympathised Ding. "What made your mother choose her anyway, Lihan? She has a quick temper and one of her ear-lobes is broken," he went on critically.

"My mother has been watching her work and she says she is strong and works well," sighed Lihan. "Another thing, her mother is a friend of my mother's, and my mother thinks that might help when they discuss her coming to live in our room."

Ding nodded understandingly. It was the custom that when married, the boy went to live with the girl's family, but sometimes the families would come to other arrangements. "Never mind," said Ding, "her parents might not agree at all."

"If they don't, I suppose my mother will look for somebody else," Lihan answered gloomily. "She is keen on having someone to help her."

Ding felt sorry for Lihan. His own betrothal had been arranged from babyhood and he had grown up with the idea that he would one day marry Usun. He was used to the idea and he liked Usun. Lihan would have to get used to his parent's choice.

"Let me go! I don't like you!" The boys turned quickly to see Anyi's sister trying to pick Imang up. The little boy was struggling and kicking. "You've got horrible lumpy ears," he yelled.

Anyi's sister had been treating Imang with good humour, but her eyes blazed with anger at his reference to her ears. She shook him hard. "You come with me," she stormed, "I'll . . ."

Ding stepped in at this point. He quickly snatched Imang from her, taking her by surprise. "My brother doesn't want to go with you," he said coldly.

Anyi's sister looked at Ding angrily. "He will come with me in the end whether he likes it or not. My father will see to that!" Turning quickly, she left them.

Imang looked relieved. "She said she wanted me to go and sit in her father's room for a little while, Ding," said the little boy. "She said, later on I will be going to live with her and she wants me to get used to her. I don't want to live with her," he ended emphatically.

"Of course you won't live with her, Imang," said Ding, "we wouldn't let you go." But he spoke with more assurance than he felt.

Four days later, the witch-doctor paid Ding's family a visit. They had been four days of apprehension for Ding. He had wanted to tell his father of Anyi's scheming, but his father was still suffering the effects of the feast and his uncertain temper kept his family at a distance.

Anyi's sister had returned to her home down-river, leaving her father to make arrangements for the adoption of Imang. The arrangements must be made according to the slow, but very thorough custom of their tribe.

"Sit down, this is your room," said Ding's father. His face was a mask of politeness and showed nothing of his surprise at this unexpected visit.

Ding knew that like most people, his father disliked and feared the witch-doctor. However, no matter what one's feelings were, guests must be greeted and treated with courtesy. Anyi had come with his father and his self-satisfied smirk suggested that he was going to enjoy himself.

As they all sat down, Ding's mother emerged from the tilung with bamboo mugs of rice beer.

"Drink some beer," said Ding's father. "It is bad beer; I'm sorry we have nothing else to give you."

"It is very good beer," replied the witch-doctor politely.

After several more polite remarks about the quality of the beer, the man talked about canoes, rice, pigs, fowls, land—anything but the object of his visit. The two boys sat silent. The one was obviously enjoying the situation, the other was in a state of mental torture.

Ding sensed his father's perplexity as he talked. It would be very bad manners to ask the witch-doctor why he had come. They must keep up an exchange of small talk until such time as the visitor was ready to reveal the purpose of his visit. Slowly and carefully, the witch-doctor led the conversation around to his daughter— and, often speaking in parables, he divulged the purpose of his visit.

Ding's father's expression never changed, but his whole body seemed to stiffen. Casually, as though he were discussing a pig or a fowl, he discussed the little boy who was the pride and joy of his heart. Often using the same parabolic speech as the witch-doctor, he graciously, nevertheless very firmly, refused to allow his son to be adopted.

Abruptly the conversation was back into more mundane channels. After a few minutes of this, the witch-doctor announced his intention of going.

"Come again. This is your room," said Ding's father.

The two visitors rose to their feet.

"Sit well, all of you."

"Go well, you two," was the polite rejoinder.

After they had gone, Ding's mother, who had been sitting listening, looked at her husband fearfully.

"The dog!" exclaimed Ding's father, slamming his fist against the wall. "Give Imang to his daughter? Never!"

Ding took his parang down from where it hung on the antlers. "I'm going to collect wood," he said abruptly and went out, leaving his parents sitting in gloomy silence. Ding knew, as they did, that this was only the beginning. The witch-doctor would come again and again with the same request. He would gradually become more threatening—though always polite. In spite of his father's resolute words, Ding knew he was profoundly shaken.

"What's the matter, Ding? You look as though you are going to kill someone."

Ding looked around and Lihan fell into step with him.

"I would like to," said Ding vehemently. "Come and get some wood and I'll tell you what's happened."

"Good," said Lihan. "I'll just go and get my parang and paddle."

Getting out into the jungle and telling Lihan about the witch-doctor's visit was a relief to Ding. Lihan listened well and understood. As Ding came to the end of his story, Lihan tugged at his hair. "I don't know how you will stop him getting his way in the end," he said.

They sat down on a log with their load of wood beside them. Ding hacked at the ground with his parang. "That's what worries me," he said glumly. "And Anyi hinted that this was only the beginning. What's the beast going to do next?"

Lihan frowned. "There are so many things he can do." Lihan had no false words of comfort; he knew the seriousness of the situation.

Picking up their loads of wood, they made their way back to their canoe.

"Did you hear about the Kelabits passing by this morning?" asked Lihan, as they stacked their wood into the canoe.

Ding looked surprised. "No. What were they doing down this way?"

"Going to trade at Long Kayo. They only stopped for a minute. Nyipa was talking to them, and he said they were telling about the white man's God."

"The white man's God?" exclaimed Ding.

"Yes. They said some of their tribe, and all the Murut tribe, have started to follow."

"The Muruts!" Ding's voice was full of contempt. "Who are they to follow a God?"

Lihan shrugged. Neither boy had seen a Murut, but both knew they were scorned by all as a degraded and debased tribe.

"The Kelabits didn't say any more about the Muruts, but they said they themselves had sent a message to the white men or missionaries, as they called them, to come and tell them about this God."

"What's the white man's God like?"

"I don't know. These fellows didn't know much. Nyipa asked them to stop on their way back. I think he is going to ask the chief to get them to invite the white men here."

"He'll never do it," said Ding. "As he said before, it's better to stick to the omens you do know without getting tangled up in a lot you don't know. I wonder if there are witch-doctors in the white man's religion?'' he added as an afterthought.

Sometimes in the next few weeks Ding wondered if after all it might not be better to enquire about the white man's God. The witch-doctor paid three more very courteous visits to Ding's room. Ding's father remained politely adamant, but Ding knew that he was worried. The whole family were, except Imang. He was aware of what was going on, but rested on the knowledge that his family had the answer to every problem—which was why he came straight to Ding when Anyi took his canoe.

It was the toy canoe that Ding had made him and from which he was seldom parted. Tearfully, he told Ding how Anyi had taken it from him and told him not to worry, for he could have it back when he went to live with his sister.

"Get it, Ding. I'm not going to live with his old sister!"

"I—I can't go just now, little brother—I'll get it later."

Imang looked disappointed. He had expected his big, brave brother to rush out as before and push Anyi over the verandah rail again. Miserably, Ding sensed his disappointment. What could he do? He didn't dare go out and have more words with Anyi.

"You're not doing anything. Go now," Imang pouted.

"I'm tired," Ding told him. "You know I have been weeding at the farm all day. I'll get it later."

"Perhaps he'll forget about it," he thought, knowing in his heart there was no hope of that. Imang wandered away discontentedly, and Ding tried to think how he could get the canoe back without a fuss.

Anyi had been away weeding on his farm for the past few weeks, and Ding had seen little of him. Now he was back and out to make trouble. "What can I do?" muttered Ding to himself. Suddenly a new and unpleasant thought occurred to him.

Why did Anyi want the toy canoe? Was it just to annoy him? What if, with something of Imang's in his possession, he could weave a charm that would make his parents want to give Imang away? Impossible! Or was it!

Ding forgot his tiredness. He sat up alert and thoughtful. He must get that canoe back.

Anyi would have it in his room, of course. Perhaps he could creep in and get it at night while everyone slept. He knew Anyi slept on the platform in his room with his younger brother. What if the canoe was in the tilung — no, it would probably be in the room. He got up. He would go and talk it over with Lihan.

"It's taking an awful risk," was Lihan's comment. "The doors will be barred and you'll have to crawl over the wall. Then you'll want to know where the canoe is and it'll be pitch dark." He shuddered. "I don't like going into that room in the day, let alone the night."

"I'll just have to do it," said Ding. "I must get that canoe."

"I'll tell you what," said Lihan, brightening a little. "I'll visit Taman Lahei, who lives next door to Anyi, and see if I can look through a crack in the wall or through the door and see the canoe; then I can tell you where it is."

"That will be a help," replied Ding.

The two boys parted, Lihan to go and spy, Ding to fret and worry.

Lihan was later able to tell Ding that the canoe was sitting on top of a rice basket standing in a corner of the room. The thought of trying to get it terrified Ding, but he knew he must try.

"Have you got my canoe yet?" were Imang's last words before he went to sleep.

"I'll go and get it later and give it to you in the morning," Ding comforted him, and with that Imang had to be satisfied.

It was after midnight when Ding thought it safe to start

off on his venture. He sat up. Lihan stirred beside him. "Are you going now?" "Yes." Ding's voice seemed to have become lost in the husky lump in his throat.

"Go well," said Lihan dolefully.

Ding slipped off the platform. The lump of fear in his throat seemed to grow bigger as he groped his way along the wall of the tilung and into the little passage. He lifted the wooden bar off the door. It slipped from his nervous fingers and fell to the floor with a clatter. There came a pause in the snoring from the tilung, followed by much coughing and spluttering, and then the steady rhythmic snore once more.

If only he could go through the rooms! What was the use of thinking about that—not one person would leave a door unbarred, let alone the whole long-house. He would have to climb over the wall. On the verandah, the darkness all around him, he began to make his way slowly along. What was that? He stopped. The soft chattering squeak of a tiny lizard rose and fell, and died away.

That was a bad omen. He would have to go back. What about the canoe? What if it were really being used as a sort of charm? He swallowed. The lump in his throat nearly choked him. He would have to ignore the omen.

Creak! Plop! Creak! The noise of a loose board beneath his feet seemed to shatter the silence. He pressed on. Something soft and furry brushed his feet. He gave a muffled exclamation of horror and stood frozen to the spot. His knees threatened to collapse beneath him. With paralysing intensity he remembered "the hairy ghost," which attacked suddenly and sucked all the blood away. Every hair on Ding's head seemed to stiffen. He wanted to run, but his legs would not move.

A soft, whimpering sound brought him out of his panic-stricken trance. He breathed again. A pup! It must have wandered away from its mother. Where was he? Was it eight pounding platforms he had to pass or seven?

"Eight, I think," he muttered to himself. This was nine. This should be Anyi's room. If only it had been a moon-lit night. He tried not to think of the hairy ghost, though he was sure it must be waiting somewhere to attack him.

He started to climb. The board creaked and groaned. He paused. The only sound was a whistling snore from inside the tilung.

Lowering himself to the floor, he felt his way along the wall. The basket should be in the corner straight ahead. A tiny light danced suddenly before his eye—he stepped back. It was a firefly. He stretched out a hand. That was the basket! His hand closed on the canoe.

"Ouch!" The canoe dropped from his hand.

"What was that?" Anyi's younger brother sat up.

Ding crouched against the basket.

"Rats," came Anyi's sleepy mumble.

"It was a funny noise for a rat." The boy lay back.

Ding sucked at his hand. There must have been a centi-pede on the canoe. As he waited for the boys to settle down again, his eyes tried to pierce the darkness. He wondered fearfully if there were any spirits watching him—he felt sure the room was crowded with them. Perhaps they were just waiting for him to get up. Perhaps —he mustn't think like that.

The canoe . . . where was the canoe? He crawled around feeling for it, hoping the centipede was gone. At last he found it, and began to make his stealthy way back. It seemed as though two nights had passed by the time he reached Lihan's room.

Ding lay down, the canoe grasped in his hand.

"You've got it," whispered Lihan.

Ding grunted an assent through chattering teeth. "You've got fever," said Lihan as the whole platform began to shake with Ding's shivering. Ding didn't tell him it was fear and not fever. The ordeal he had just experienced had shattered his self-control.

"What's the use! What's the use! He'll win in the end. He'll win in the end."

The words seem to come from nowhere and hammer on his fear-ridden mind until he fell into a restless sleep.

Arriving at his room the next morning, those words came back with force. "What's the use! He'll win in the end."

8

DING knew as soon as he walked into the room that something was wrong. Mujan was lying on the platform sobbing. His father sat silent and obviously grief stricken, hugging a bewildered Imang.

From the tilung came a soft moaning wail. Glancing in, he saw his mother sitting by the fire, rocking to and fro in her distress.

"What's the matter?" Ding asked, his face white and drawn.

"Your mother had a dream."

"A dream!" Ding's legs seemed to give under him. He sat down heavily. A dream! What's the use? He'll get his own way in the end. Did witch-doctors have that much power? Is that why Anyi had wanted the canoe? "A dream!" he groaned. There was no need to ask what kind of a dream. He knew what had happened.

If someone had a dream in which a child was given away, or someone came and asked for it, in real life the child must be given to the person in the dream. If this was not carried out, the child would die.

There would be no further talks with the witch-doctor about Imang's adoption. When Anyi's sister came to collect him after harvest, he would be given to her without ado. They must bend to the inevitable.

"You've got my canoe." Imang struggled out of his father's arms and went over to Ding.

Ding had forgotten the canoe. His night adventure had been in vain, but at least it gave Imang some pleasure to have the canoe back.

"We must go to the farm," his father said woodenly.

Somehow they rallied themselves and set off for the farm with Lihan and his family, who shared in their grief.

They were a silent and melancholy group as they poled up river. Nor was their mood improved when a honey-bird flew in front of them just before they reached the farm. A bad omen! Wearily they turned back. Another day wasted! Another day when the monkeys and sparrows would eat freely of the ripening grain! Another day for the weeds to grow unhindered.

Back at the house, the men settled down to splicing jungle rope. They were going to need a lot if the long-house was to be moved.

Ding and Lihan sat in their usual place, working together. The long-house was comparatively deserted. Most people were at their farms. There was the usual sprinkling of old people and children, also some who, like themselves, had had to come home because of omens.

"We will have to find another tree to make a canoe, Ding," said Lihan, by way of breaking the silence.
Ding merely grunted.

"I just heard our fathers talking about making one too," Lihan went on, "both our present ones are getting old."

"What's the use," was Ding's morose reply, "we might get another one nearly finished and then have to throw it away." He sounded as though a canoe had never been completed in his lifetime.

Lihan looked at him anxiously. Ding's moroseness worried him. He knew the dream had been a heavy blow, and he could understand the family grief, but there was something about Ding that he didn't understand.

"He's looking awfully thin," he thought. "We all are, for that matter; I guess that's to be expected. Food is scarce. No, it's not just thinness, he's gaunt and haggard and he looks sort of—of haunted. Yes, that's it, haunted and hunted."

"A fine little lad, isn't he?" They both looked up, first at the leering Anyi, and then at the object of his remark —Imang.

Ding looked down quickly and went on working with hands which shook with hardly-contained anger.

"You beast," thought Lihan, and hated himself for not having the courage to say so. "Any more news of the white man?" he asked abruptly, ignoring the other's remark.

Anyi raised a scornful eyebrow. "Not a hope of him coming," he drawled, "my father doesn't approve."

Lihan well knew that the Kelabits had long since returned home. Nyipa had been unsuccessful in his attempt to interest the chief in the white man's God. Ding and Lihan strongly suspected that he had been more than persuaded by the head witch-doctor to ignore Nyipa's advice, and Anyi's words confirmed their suspicions.

"There's talk of having a long-house meeting to discuss it."

There was a note of defiance in Lihan's voice. He knew that more and more people were thinking of what Nyipa had to say.

"Makes no difference," was the confident reply. There was a strained pause. Anyi rose to his feet. "You're looking ill, Ding," he remarked. "I hope you will be all right." His tone belied the sincerity of his words. "One never knows—sit well, you two." As he started to saunter off he said, "Oh, my father may be down to see your father sometime, Ding. I'm looking around for a wife, you know."

As he swaggered away, Ding and Lihan looked at one another. "He wouldn't," gasped Lihan.

"Yes, he would." Lihan found the calm hopelessness of Ding's reply rather frightening. Ding rose: "I've got a fearful headache. I think I'll go and lie down."

Lihan watched him go down the verandah and disappear through a doorway. "I don't like it," he muttered to himself, "I don't like it at all."

Ding stumbled into the blackness of the tilung and flung himself on the floor. First Imang and now Mujan. Mujan married to that fiend? He shuddered. Of course, his parents wouldn't consent. He laughed a little hysterically. That's what he had said about Imang—wouldn't allow it. They always get their own way in the end. What had the fool meant by saying he looked sick? "One never knows" —what had he meant by that? What was he going to do? You don't argue with the witch-doctor. "My head! My head!" he groaned.

When Mujan came in from the afternoon feeding of the pigs, she found her brother rolling around on the floor muttering to himself. She ran to the room next door where Imang was playing. "Imang, go and tell our mother to come. Quickly!" she added as he showed signs of arguing.

It was soon apparent that Ding had a bad attack of fever and a witch-doctor was called immediately. It was one of the women witch-doctors, a thin rake of a woman with shrivelled features and no teeth.

A mat was laid on the floor of the tilung and a small stool placed in the middle. On this the witch-doctor sat, silent and unmoving, in the darkness. Suddenly she rose to her feet. Crouching at Ding's head, she started to blow on him, all the way down to his feet. In a little while, she began to make clutching movements at Ding's body. She was throwing the sickness out by the handful, she explained to a large audience who were now crowded into the tilung—not that anyone could see what she was doing, for it was pitch dark. She now pronounced the boy cured and, after collecting a fat fee in beads, went on her way.

In spite of her ministrations and predictions, Ding's condition grew steadily worse. Everyone sat around him and talked in worried voices. In a vain attempt to relieve his headache, Mujan sat beside him, pinching the flesh of his forehead until it was a mass of red weals.

Finally, the witch-doctor had to be called again. "This is indeed a very bad sickness," she explained. A pig would have to be killed. Ding's family could ill afford a pig; yet, for his sake they willingly gave one. The witch-doctor then demanded that some Illah fish be brought, with rice and leaves. On being told that there was neither rice nor fish available, she replied that she herself had some and would use that—but of course, it would be costly.

The throat of the pig was now cut and some of the blood rubbed on Ding's arm. Following this, some of the flesh was cut away from the throat of the pig and mixed in with the rice and fish. This mixture was divided into small portions and wrapped in the leaves. Having completed the last bundle, the witch-doctor rose and commenced to put two little bundles in each of the things that pertained to the life of the family—two in the basket containing the family wealth of beads, two over the fire, two in the basket used for pig food—on everything and into everything they went, while the witch-doctor muttered unceasingly an unintelligible string of words.

Meanwhile, Ding's fever raged. The little tilung and the room outside, shook with the force of the rigors that wracked him.

When at times he seemed to indicate that he had a pain in his chest, the faithful Mujan began to pinch the flesh of that area, making more of the red weals that she hoped would relieve his sickness.

After the witch-doctor had left, everyone waited hopefully for him to improve, but instead, he grew steadily worse, and the talk became louder and more distracted. As for Ding, he was unaware of the witch-doctor's ministrations, or of the concern he was giving his family and friends. He was away in another world of leering faces, that kept saying; "It's no use. You can't argue with the witch-doctors. They'll get their own way in the end." Stark horror swept over him as unseen hands seemed to be pulling him into oblivion. "No! No!" he would scream as he felt himself going. Coming out of a rigor he would find that he was still there, and then it would start all over again.

On the third day, the witch-doctor called in another witch-doctor for consultation and between them they made it known that Ding might die. "He must have offended the spirits very much, otherwise he would have responded to the 'treatment'," they said.

As they did not lower their voices, the half-conscious Ding, about to slip into the terrifying blackness once more, heard their conversation. Spasms of terror shook him. He was going to die. He was going to die. He was going out into the unknown. It was no use—no use.

"The white man's God." He heard the words from afar, and, "They've gone to get him". Ding seemed to be suspended somewhere—"Is that what they were saying?" He tried to listen, but so many people were talking in the little room and all about different things.

"The white man's God—what if He were stronger than the spirits? Stronger than the witch-doctors? He could get even with Anyi then; he'd kill him, that's what he'd do—and the spirits wouldn't be able to touch him."

"Drink this." He recognised his mother's voice, and drank. Whatever it was, it was bitter. He wanted to be sick.

"I won't die," he said to himself. "I won't die. I'll wait

for the white man's God and then I'll get even with Anyi."

It was later, when he was able to speak, that Ding heard that four men had left with the Kelabits to contact the white man and ask him to come and tell them about his God. It was the Kelabits who had provided the bitter medicine. They said the white man had given it to them and it had great power against fever.

Ding was encouraged by all this news. Even if the God Himself wasn't coming, this white man must know Him and must himself be quite powerful.

9

"THE men have arrived back, Ding."

"Did they bring the white man?"

"No, but they brought his promise to come in thirty days."

"Thirty days!"

"Yes, I saw the piece of knotted jungle vine. There were twenty-one knots left in it as it took them nine days to get home."

"What news did they bring of the white man's God?"

"Good news," Lihan grinned, "there are no witch-doctors in the white man's religion, no omens, and their God is more powerful than all the spirits."

"Ah," sighed Ding with satisfaction. That was good news indeed.

"What has Anyi's father got to say?"

"Quite a lot. He's furious. He said the spirits are angry and will wipe out the whole village if we are not careful."

"What is everyone else saying?"

"Some are scared, especially the women; some are pretty sceptical about the white man and his God, and others are just waiting to see what's going to happen next."

"What more do you know about this white man's God?"

"Nothing, really. There is to be a meeting tonight and the four men are to tell us all they know. Apparently the white man sent back a special message."

"Come and tell me all they say, Lihan."

"Of course I will. It's a pity you can't come and hear for yourself."

He looked at Ding's weak and emaciated body. Poor Ding, he could not even sit up yet.

"I'll have to go now, Ding. The others should be home any time. Sit well."

After he had gone, Ding waited impatiently for his family to come home. No one had been able to go to the farm while he had been sick. Even now someone from his own family or Lihan's must stay with him and care for him.

It distressed him to think of the havoc the monkeys and birds had been causing while he had been ill, and to know that even now the farm must lack the help of two people. If only he could get strong quickly!

"Ding, look, I caught it myself." A small and smelly fish was dangled under his nose.

"Ah, you are home, my little brother, and such a fine fish you have caught."

"Yes, and I brought it back for you. Our mother wanted to cook it this morning when I caught it, but I wanted you to see it as it really is."

"You are a very thoughtful little boy and very kind to your sick brother." Ding patted him affectionately.

"I'm going to the meeting tonight, Ding, and I will come and tell you all about it."

"Good," said Ding, "I won't feel so badly about not going then."

The meeting, like most long-house meetings, went on till the early hours of the morning. In his weakness, Ding slept most of the time. Nevertheless, in his wakeful moments, he was impatient for the meeting to end.

At last Lihan came. The others lingered on, discussing all they had heard till it was time to go to work.

Ding looked up eagerly as Lihan entered. He seemed to be carrying something. As he came into the tiny ring of light cast by the tree-gum lamp, Ding could see that it was the sleeping Imang. Lihan put his small burden on the platform and sat down.

"What happened?" asked Ding expectantly.

"The men had some strange things to tell, Ding."

"Strange! Were they bad things?"

"No, not bad, just strange."

"Tell me."

"I will tell you the two messages the white man sent."

"He sent two messages?"

"Yes. He made the men repeat them over and over again so they wouldn't forget or get them wrong. The first message was this. 'Tell your people that the God I serve is the only true God. He is the God of all men, of every colour and of every language.'"

Ding was silent for a minute. "They are good words, Lihan. What was his other message?"

Lihan wrinkled his brow. "The second message is the strange one—a nice sort of strange—it's hard to explain."

"Tell me," said Ding impatiently.

"The men said that this message is actually from a book of God's words."

"God's words?"

"Yes. The men said the missionary made them sit down with a Kelabit who knew both our language and the Malay language and translated these words from the Book he has."

"Is it a very big book?"

"I don't know, but they say he reads it a lot. Anyway, after he had translated this verse, he made them repeat it over and over again until they couldn't forget it, and told them it was the message he would be bringing to us. I too have learnt it by heart."

"Tell me these words."

"God so loved the world that He gave His only begotten Son that whosoever believeth in Him should not perish but have everlasting life."

Ding looked at him in astonishment. "Say those words again."

Lihan repeated them.

"What do they mean?"

"The men asked the missionary, and he said they meant

exactly what they said. He told them a most wonderful story about the Son of God, whose name is Jesus Christ. They said we must wait for the missionary to come and tell the story, because we wouldn't believe them."

"It is all very strange," mused Ding. "It will be interesting to hear what the missionary has to say."

The coming of the missionary was the main topic of conversation night and day. There were many different opinions about the messages he had sent, though everyone agreed that they were good messages—except of course, the head witch-doctor and some of his colleagues. They could not see a very rosy future in a religion which had no witch-doctors.

Imang was very enthusiastic about the coming of the missionary. He asked endless questions as to the appearance of the white man.

Was the white man like the flowers in the jungle, or dirty white like the dogs? Was his hair white too, and did he have two legs, arms, eyes and so on? The main answer to all his questions from the weary receivers of them was an unsatisfactory: "Wait and see".

At last the big day arrived. No one knew just when the missionary would get there, but Imang and his friends went at the crack of dawn and climbed a tree on the bend of the river. They sat there until the middle of the day when an excited, "He's coming!" from one of their group sent them all flying to the long-house to spread the news.

Like most of the young folk, Ding hung back among the trees and watched from a distance. The women peered shyly over the verandah rails. It was only the chief, the committee men and some of the elders who actually went forward to meet the missionary.

Imang and company crept up behind rocks and had a better view than most.

Later, in their room, Imang gave a first hand account of the white man close up. "Ding, he smiled at me, honest he did. I ducked down behind a rock and when I looked up he smiled again, and called out—'Don't be frightened.' Does he know our language?"

"No, he knows just a few words."

"What's the matter with his feet?"

"His feet?"

"Yes, he's got them all covered up. Are they sick?"

"Oh," Ding laughed, "white men don't walk about in their bare feet. They always wear those things."

He spoke with the superior air of one who knew such things, but in fact he had only just found it out himself from old Nyipa.

Imang's eyes grew as big as saucers. "Do they? It must be awfully uncomfortable. You should have seen the way he walked up the notched pole—just like a monkey! And Ding, he's not white at all, he's sort of pink; why do they call him white? Oh, and did you see his eyes? Such funny ones, blue like the sky. Why are they blue?"

Ding laughed. "What a lot of questions."

"There are lots more. What is . . ."

Ding put his hand over his mouth. "Not another one, my little fellow. Go and ask your father, he's more likely to know all the answers."

"I wanted to, but he was too busy talking to Anyi's father."

"Anyi's father!" The smile died on Ding's face. "What about?"

"Don't know, I think his daughter—you know, the one with the horrible ears I'm not going to live with," Imang explained confusedly.

"Where are they?"

"On the verandah."

Ding got up and went out. He saw his father and the witch-doctor sitting talking. Outwardly it seemed a friendly conversation, but Ding could tell by the upright way his father was sitting that he was annoyed.

He went in through one of the doorways and walked

back through the rooms to his own room. "What was the witch-doctor talking about?" he wondered.

Ding's father was one of the men who had joined Nyipa's ranks of enthusiasts and were advocating that they follow the only True God, as they now called Him. Therefore, he came into the category of those who particularly angered the witch-doctor and his followers.

The verandah door opened and his father came in, looking worried and angry. He saw the question in Ding's eyes. "He wants to send for his daughter straight away to come and get Imang. He said that ever since he heard of your mother's dream he had been worried about the boy."

"It's customary to wait a while after a dream before giving the child away," said Ding quickly.

"Of course it is," replied his father. "The man is afraid we will follow the True God and not give the lad over."

"You wouldn't think of disobeying the dream?"

"I don't know. From all I have heard about the True God, He would understand and help us."

"Have you heard more?"

"Not much. The white man is going to tell us all about Him tonight."

"Did Anyi's father say anything about Mujan?"

"He did, curse him! Anyway, he can't do anything about that now. It will have to go through the usual channels and finally be discussed by the whole house. By that time, things may have changed."

"I hope so," replied Ding.

Reason had told him that to kill Anyi would only bring trouble to himself and his family. However, he planned to give him a thorough hiding. His thoughts were full of plans for his revenge: "I'll terrorise him for the rest of his life—just as he has terrorised me."

They must find out as quickly as possible how to get in touch with the True God though, or Imang would be lost to them.

10

"LET us not wait. Let us follow now."

"We must be very careful, my son. This is something bigger than I imagined. It is not to be taken lightly."

"But, father, we will be free of all the spirits, the omens and the witch-doctors."

"Ah, yes. But is that enough? The Book which the missionary has tells us that the True God is holy and righteous, powerful and just. These are mighty words— no, we cannot follow such a One lightly."

"But the missionary said God is happy to release us from all these things."

"True. However, we must remember that God paid a great price to set us free—not just from our fears, but from the root of them—sin." Ding looked at his father. He had never seen him so thoughtful. "For God so loved the world, that He gave His only begotten Son, that whosoever believeth in Him should not perish, but have everlasting life." The older man said the words over slowly to himself. "Such words, such wonderful words."

Ding tugged at his hair. "I'll go and look for Lihan," he thought. "Father seems to be in a trance or something."

He found Lihan on the verandah gazing over the rail. "Where's the missionary?" he asked.

"Up behind the house, sitting on a rock," replied Lihan.

"All by himself?"

"Yes. They say that he goes away by himself every morning early and reads God's words and talks to Him."

"This custom sounds good to me," remarked Ding.

Lihan didn't reply for a moment. "Yes," he said finally, "the Lord Jesus Christ must be really worth following."

Ding looked at him. "What's wrong with everyone?" he thought. "Lihan is acting just like my father."

The meeting last night had certainly been up to expectations, but he could not understand this strange attitude of his father and Lihan.

The Lord Jesus Christ! Apparently He was the Son meant in that verse. Ding tried to recall what the missionary had said: Something about dying on a Cross. He had not really been listening to that bit. He had been busy thinking up a couple of ways he could torment Anyi.

He'd got the bit about the Lord Jesus Christ having defeated Satan. Satan—he was the head of all evil and was their present master. How could they throw him over and follow after this Lord Jesus who would protect them from Satan?

"I must check up on how He protects us," mused Ding. "I would hate to give Anyi a hiding and then find I didn't have His protection."

"He must have had a lot of courage to speak so boldly to all those men."

What on earth was Lihan talking about? "Who?"

"The Lord Jesus Christ. And yet when they nailed Him on the Cross He asked for them to be forgiven. That would take a lot of love, and a lot of courage too." Lihan seemed to be in another world.

"I guess so." Ding could not think of anything else to say. "I'll go and see the missionary," he said, "and just get this custom straight. Sit well, Lihan."

"Go well," said Lihan, from his other world.

Ding walked down the verandah. As he was about to descend the notched pole, he met Anyi coming up. "Ah, the noble Ding! You're still with us, I see. You're very thin. You must be careful, Ding."

"Huh," thought Ding, "at least Anyi is his usual beastly self. Nothing could change him."

He descended the notched pole without so much as acknowledging the other's presence. "My turn's coming," he muttered to himself, "then we'll see who's going to be careful."

From the back of the long-house he could see the missionary sitting on a rock on the mountainside. He looked around. One of the Kelabits who had come with the missionary was walking towards the house. Ding hailed him. "Will you come with me and help me to talk to the missionary?" he asked.

The Kelabit looked dubious. "He's busy talking with God, I think."

"Oh, he won't mind. Come and help me," insisted Ding, knowing the Kelabit would be too polite to refuse. They went up to the rock together, and the Kelabit said something to the missionary. He smiled at Ding. "Sit down," he invited. It was one of the few expressions he knew in the Kayan language.

At first Ding talked rather shyly about the river and the rapids and other mundane things. He had been busy thinking about getting this Christian custom straight in his mind. He had not stopped to consider that talking to this strange man—and that through an interpreter— might be rather difficult.

After a suitable time had elapsed, during which they talked about nothing in particular, Ding launched somewhat hesitantly into the purpose of his visit.

"Is it true," he asked, "that the Lord Jesus Christ is more powerful than Satan?" "Yes," replied the missionary, "it is true."

"And if we throw over our present beliefs, we need not be frightened of the witch-doctors or anything?"

The white man looked at him thoughtfully for a minute, in a way which made Ding feel a little uncomfortable. "Why do you ask?"

The question came as a surprise to Ding. "Huh! Uhh!

I want to be sure. After all, the witch-doctors are threatening us." He added the latter information a little impatiently. Why didn't the missionary answer his question?

"Do you want to know the Lord Jesus Christ, Ding?" was the next seemingly pointless question.

"Why, of course I do. My father is one of the men who is encouraging people to follow Him," replied Ding proudly.

"Do you know why the Lord Jesus Christ was crucified?"

"Umm—to release us from evil."

"What do you understand by evil?"

"Huh! Uhh! All these omens and spirits and witch-doctors—and their sons." The last words seemed to come of their own accord.

The missionary looked interested. "Witch-doctors' sons are evil too, are they?"

"Some of them," replied Ding. He must be fair to those who were quite decent. "Those like Anyi . . ." Before he knew what he was doing, he was telling the missionary all about Anyi.

The white man listened. "I guess you would say that Anyi has a lot of sin in his heart," was his comment as Ding finished his somewhat lengthy tirade.

"Oh, lots." Ding couldn't think of a word strong enough to describe Anyi's heart.

"How about you?"

"Me!" Ding looked at him in astonishment. "What do you mean? Oh, I'm not like Anyi." Ding felt relieved. Of course, the missionary did not know him. It was only natural that he should ask a few questions.

The missionary turned the pages of his book. "You know, Ding, it says in this Book, 'All have sinned and come short of the glory of God.' Do you think that could include you?"

Ding felt uneasy—this conversation was not going according to plan—not his plan anyway. "It says 'all' so I guess it includes me," he said somewhat sullenly.

"You hate Anyi, don't you?"

"Very much."

"Do you think hate could be called sin?"

"You don't understand just what a beast Anyi is."

"Answer my question." The missionary's voice was kind, but firm.

"I guess so." Ding seemed to be doing a lot of guessing this morning.

"You know, Ding, what you want to do is to throw over the power of this custom, so that you can do to Anyi what he has been doing to you. In other words, you want to change your custom, but not your master." Ding was silent. The missionary went on: "This Book tells us that God won't help us if we hang on to our sin, but He will show us how to get rid of it. God won't help you to hate Anyi—He'll show you how to love him."

"Love Anyi!" The words shocked Ding out of his silence.

"Yes. A minute ago you called him a beast."

"And so he is."

"Has it occurred to you that in the sight of God you might be a beast too? Aren't the things that are in Anyi's heart in yours too—things like hate and pride and anger?"

His heart the same as Anyi's! The thought repelled Ding. "I'm not a bit like Anyi," he thought, "the other boys like me and they don't like Anyi. The older men like me too, because I'm helpful and a good leader. Anyi's not like that. No, I'm not like Anyi. This man just doesn't understand."

"It is time for me to go and help my father," Ding said abruptly.

"Think on the things I have told you, Ding. Ask God to help you understand," counselled the missionary, as Ding rose to go.

"Sit well," were Ding's parting words.

Walking slowly down the mountainside, Ding thought

over all that the missionary had said. It hadn't been a very satisfactory conversation. He had confirmed that the Lord Jesus was more powerful than Satan, but would the Lord Jesus help him to have his revenge on Anyi? "God won't help you to hate Anyi. He will show you how to love him." That is what the missionary had said. "Who wants to love Anyi?" muttered Ding to himself. "You look worried Ding." Anyi's familiar sneer brought him to a halt. "Of course you ought to be worried," Anyi went on smoothly, "the spirits are angry."

Hatred welled up in Ding's heart. Throwing all caution to the wind he faced Anyi. "We will see about that," he glowered. "The Lord Jesus is greater than the spirits. When we follow Him, you will be the one to be worried."

Anyi laughed scornfully. "Your missionary friend will go off and leave you soon," he said, "then we will see how powerful this Lord Jesus is."

A chill ran up Ding's spine. If the missionary didn't stay—what then?

"That is only your talk," he said with all the bravado he could muster. "I'm going to follow this Lord Jesus even if it is only to get even with you. Then we will see who is the stronger."

Anyi's eyes narrowed. No one had ever spoken to him like that. "I tell you, Ding," he almost spat the words out, "whatever is decided, the spirits will still win. Wait till the missionary leaves and we will show you."

Hatred overcame fear, and Ding was about to strike Anyi, when a gentle cough made them aware that the missionary and the interpreter had followed Ding down the mountainside.

Without another word Anyi brushed past the two men. Ding's angry eyes met those of the missionary. A sense of shame swept over him. He turned and stumbled toward the long-house.

11

"WHAT is the matter, Ding?" asked Lihan anxiously as he met Ding coming up the notched pole. "You look . . ." His words trailed off as Ding pushed past him with a muttered, "Nothing."

Arriving at his room, Ding was relieved to find the members of his family out at their various tasks. He sat in the darkness of the tilung and tried to sort out his confused thoughts. He was shaken as he considered the depths of his hatred for Anyi. "Aren't the things that are in Anyi's heart in yours too—things like hate and pride and anger?" He squirmed within himself. "Could the missionary have been right after all?"

"But what could you do with a fellow like Anyi? 'God will show you how to love him,' the missionary had said. Could God really do that?" He tried to think of loving Anyi. "What good would it do?" A new thought came to him. "What good did hating Anyi do, anyway?" He sighed, this was all very new and hard to understand.

Movement and murmur of voices outside told him that some of the family had returned. He rose as his mother came into the tilung. "You are here, Ding!" she exclaimed, "are you sick?"

"No. I'm not sick," replied Ding.

"Your father has been looking for you everywhere," scolded his mother. "He wants you to go and get some wood."

Without another word, Ding gathered up his parang and went in search of his father.

That evening Ding and Lihan joined the men who had gathered in the chief's room to question the missionary and to discuss whether or not they would follow this Lord Jesus Christ.

The young people would have no say, but a few like Ding and Lihan hung around the doors, curious to hear the discussion. A sprinkling of old women could be seen on the fringe of the crowd. Women folk had no say either, but these were mainly witch-doctors and could voice an opinion if they liked.

"Aiyow! Listen to Anyi's father," whispered Ding.

"Are you mad? Do you think you can defy the spirits? The spirits will bring trouble and sickness upon you, if you dare to follow the European," raged the witch-doctor.

"I do not want you to follow me," interjected the missionary quickly, "I am only a man. I want you to follow the Lord Jesus Christ."

"Our ancestors have followed the spirits down through the ages," continued the witch-doctor, ignoring the missionary. "You know what they have told us about the ways of the spirits when they are defied. You know the things that have happened to us when we have disobeyed them."

A shudder went through the listeners. "The witch-doctor speaks truly," murmured one old cronie to another, "we know the spirits are powerful, but what do we know about this Jesus?"

"The missionary says He is stronger than the spirits," said a young man hopefully.

"How does he know?" grunted one of the older men listening to the conversation. "What has he had to do with the spirits?"

"What about the Muruts?" retorted the young man.

"Yes, look at the Muruts," murmured several people who were also following the conversation. "They have been completely changed."

"I'd like to see it," snorted a sceptic.

"I have seen it." The group turned to look at the speaker, a middle-aged man leaning against the wall.

"When?" they asked in unison.

"When I went to a Kelabit long-house to trade, some time ago," replied the man. "There was a group of Muruts there. They had come to tell the Kelabits about Jesus. I couldn't believe they were Muruts—they were so different."

"Listen to the witch-doctor, you noisy ones," growled one of the committee men.

The witch-doctor was still speaking: "If you follow, we witch-doctors won't help you when the evil spirits start tormenting you," he warned. "This European will go away with his Book and all his great promises and you will be left to their mercy."

"Will you stay with us?" asked one of the crowd, of the missionary.

"No, I cannot stay," said the missionary, "but even if I could, I am not the one you are to trust in. I have no power of my own. If you trust the Lord Jesus Christ, He will deliver you and protect you from all evil."

"All very well," muttered someone, "what if this Jesus does not want to help us, what then?"

"So Anyi was right—the missionary wasn't going to stay," thought Ding.

"Well He helped the Muruts, and I for one believe that He can help us." The words were spoken loudly and clearly. People craned to see the speaker and Ding was proud of the fact that it was his father who had spoken so courageously.

"I do too," agreed another man. "We've been tormented long enough and I am going to trust Jesus."

"Can a witch-doctor follow?" The question caused a stir.

"It's Bulan La'ing," whispered Ding to Lihan. "Remember, she never wanted to be a witch-doctor, and has always been unhappy."

"Yes," said the missionary. "The Lord Jesus died for all, witch-doctors included."

"Well, I am going to follow too," said Bulan La'ing adamantly.

A murmur of discussion arose: "If we don't have to worry about the spirits and the omens we will probably get good crops," said someone.

"Do you think the spirits are going to sleep?" asked his neighbours sarcastically. "If you ignore them they will have their revenge."

"Not if this Jesus is protecting us."

"It's a risk defying the spirits, to follow someone we don't know."

"Yes, I'm frightened to follow."

"I don't understand all this talk about sin, and this Jesus being crucified for us."

There was a stir and silence fell as the chief rose to speak. "My fathers and mothers," he commenced, politely addressing the elders. "My brothers and sisters, we have heard the message of our guest, the missionary, and we have heard the warnings of our brother the witch-doctor, and we have discussed one with another the merits of this Lord Jesus. There have been many words spoken, but we cannot go on talking. A canoe tossed from wave to wave makes little progress and is finally battered on the rocks. We must come to a decision. It has been our custom down through the ages to work, to live and to worship together. If we are to follow this Jesus, let us follow together. If we are to continue in the worship of the spirits, let us do so together. At present we are divided. We will take a short time now to consider this decision and then we will put it to the vote. Think well; think carefully."

"What do you think will happen Ding?" asked Lihan as they strolled away from the chief's room.

"I don't know," said Ding, "the chief didn't give any indication of what he thought. I guess it will depend on what he and the committee decide."

"And the witch-doctors," added Lihan. "Ouch!" he exclaimed, as Ding dug him in the ribs with his elbow. They were passing through one of the rooms on their way to Ding's room and Ding had noticed Anyi's father and several other witch-doctors sitting on a mat, deep in conversation. They didn't notice the boys.

"It may be very profitable at that." Anyi's father was rubbing his chin thoughtfully as he spoke.

"Yes, we could let it be known that we intend to remain in business," said another. "I can see it being very profitable."

The boys passed on. "What do you think they are up to?" whispered Lihan. Ding shrugged: "Nothing good, that's certain," he replied. "I wish the missionary would stay," he added.

They had arrived at Ding's room and found his sister and three other girls sitting on the platform, their eyes downcast. Not until he was half way across the room did Ding see Anyi lolling up against the wall.

"Ah, there you are, Ding," Anyi smirked, "I'm just visiting your sister."

Angry words rushed to Ding's lips, but before he spoke he remembered the missionary's words, "Jesus will show you how to love Anyi." The anger seemed to drain out of him. "My sister doesn't want you to visit her, Anyi," he said quietly. "Go well," he added politely.

For a moment Anyi stood undecided. There was something about Ding he did not understand. Finally he slouched to the door. "I'll go," he said, "but you heard what the missionary said—he can't stay. No matter what decision is made, the spirits will win in the end."

Dawn was breaking when the great decision was made. The long-house of Long Nangah had decided to become Christian.

"I don't really understand," said Ding to Lihan, "the last time we saw Anyi, a short time ago, he wasn't a Christian, I'm sure."

"Perhaps he's changed now," said Lihan, without conviction.

At that moment, the object of their conversation appeared before them. "Well, we are all Christians now, Ding," he said with a sarcastic smile, "didn't I tell you the spirits would win?" He went on his way, leaving Ding and Lihan puzzled and uncertain. What did this all mean?

12

THE long-house was a hive of activity. Now that the decision had been made, many hurried to obey the instructions of the missionary and remove from their rooms all signs of their former worship.

Ding, on his father's instructions, climbed to the top of the tilung and loosened all the branches of blood-stained leaves that were hanging there. His father and mother were gathering small pieces of bamboo tied together, little baskets of odds and ends and all kinds of miscellaneous objects from every conceivable nook and cranny. These were the "charms" gathered from time to time in various crises from the witch-doctor, at no little cost, to ensure the family against the anger of the evil spirits.

From time to time, Ding saw his father go to a corner of the tilung as if to get something. At such times, he noticed his mother stiffen and become tense, and then relax and look relieved as his father turned quickly away, empty-handed.

"Are you ready in here?" The Kelabit interpreter had entered with the missionary.

Ding's father pointed to a heap of charms in a basket, in the centre of the floor. "Is that all?" asked the missionary.

Ding's father nodded, but didn't look up. Ding sensed there was something wrong. "Are you sure that is all?" The missionary was looking straight at his father. "Remember, if you are to be a true Christian, you cannot serve two masters. You must trust the Lord Jesus wholly or not at all."

The older man coughed and looked at his wife, who had

turned pale. "There is one more," he said unsteadily, "but it is a charm of great power. I am afraid to touch it. No one but the witch-doctor has ever touched it, and he said that if it ever left this room, one of us would die."

"Do you believe this charm has more power than the Lord Jesus Christ?" The missionary's eyes went from one to the other of the family, "Do you?"

"If it has, there wouldn't be much point in trusting the Lord Jesus," said Ding half to himself.

"I'm hungry!" A little ball of humanity came flying through the door, breaking the tension and bringing a smile to the missionary's eyes.

Ding's father straightened. "You are right," he said to the missionary, "if we are to serve the Lord Jesus, we must hold nothing back." He strode to the corner of the room and untied a small bottle from the post. In the bottle was a small stone. He threw it on the heap of charms. Then picking up the basket he strode purposefully toward the door to cast them in the river.

As Ding's father went out of one door, Lihan burst in another. "Ding, I've found out what Anyi meant." In his excitement, Lihan did not see the missionary and his companion. Ding, eager to hear Lihan's news, forgot the visitors.

"Some of the witch-doctors, like Anyi's father, are going to continue on with the spirits while pretending to be Christians. They say that once the missionary goes, a lot of people will be scared and will go to the witch-doctors just the same. The witch-doctors say they will charge high fees too."

The quiet voice of the Kelabit interpreter to the missionary made both boys conscious of the presence of the visitors.

Ding looked up at the missionary. "That means that we are not really all Christians and yet everyone is called a

Christian. How will we know the difference, and can we really deceive the Lord Jesus like that?"

The missionary looked at Ding and Lihan thoughtfully.

"Once when I was visiting a Murut long-house," he began, "the chief took me to see his farm. It was almost harvest time, and as we stood looking at the ripe rice the chief told me that they were expecting the best harvest they had ever had.

"Sometime later I was visiting that long-house again and I asked the chief about the harvest, which was now over. 'A very poor harvest', he replied, 'very poor indeed'.

"'Why is that?' I asked, 'I understood you to say you expected a good harvest.' 'I did too,' said the chief, 'but when we went to harvest, we found that many of the grains were only husks—they had nothing in them'."

The missionary paused and then went on—"There are many people today who have the name of Christian, like that drunken trader you told me about, but the Lord Jesus Christ is not in them; they are like the husks—empty." He opened his Bible. "No, the Lord Jesus is not deceived by these people, Ding, for He knows what is in our hearts."

"How do I get rid of hatred in my heart?" asked Ding abruptly.

"Ask the Lord Jesus to take it away," was the simple reply.

"Can He really take it away?" wondered Ding, as the missionary moved off into the next room.

"I wish we knew more about being Christians," mused Ding's father. "It won't be easy when the missionary goes. Even though everyone is taking the name of Christian, it is obvious that not all intend to follow."

"Wouldn't it have been better if just those of us who wanted to follow had done so?" asked Ding.

"Yes, it would have been better that way," replied his father, "but we Kayans have always done things together.

Also, by turning to Christianity together, we help the ones who are of two minds. Those who didn't want to turn are really very few, and they will follow their own hearts anyway." He tugged at the strip of hair down his back. "They will do all they can to make things difficult for us."

"I know Anyi is just waiting for the missionary to go, to make trouble," said Ding.

At that moment Imang emerged from the tilung, cramming cooked rice into his mouth. "Ding, why is everyone throwing things into the river?" His words were hardly distinguishable.

"We are going to follow the Lord Jesus now, Imang." Ding spoke slowly, wanting the little boy to understand. "We have thrown all these things into the river because they belong to the evil spirits."

"Ding," Imang swallowed a big lump of rice, "I saw Widow Paya' hide some of her things and then tell the missionary she didn't have any more. I heard her tell someone she is going to be sure of protection from both sides." It was a long speech for Imang and came in breathless gulps. "Did we keep something back, just to be sure, Ding?"

"No, Imang, we didn't, because we know we can really trust the Lord Jesus."

"Will He protect me from that horrible woman with the ears?" asked Imang. "Yes, He will," Ding spoke firmly. Anyi's father would be along with his demands as soon as the missionary had gone. Ding was sure of that.

13

THE missionary had gone. Ding and his friends turned away from the river bank where they had been watching his long-boat disappear out of sight.

"When will he be back?" asked one of the boys.

"He couldn't say," answered Ding.

"Isn't there someone else he could send?"

"No. He said there isn't anyone just now."

"But don't forget he said that the Lord Jesus is with us all the time," exhorted Lihan.

"I wish we could really see the Lord Jesus," said another boy, "then we would know He really exists."

"We have never been able to see the spirits, but we know they exist," said Ding.

"That's true," replied the boy thoughtfully.

"We will soon see how real your Jesus is." The boys looked up to see Anyi standing watching them.

"We know He is real, Anyi," said Ding quietly and stepped past him.

"You know, if there is one thing that convinces me of the reality of the Lord Jesus," said Ding, as they continued on their way, "it is that I no longer hate Anyi. I asked the Lord Jesus to take the hate away, and He did."

"I wish He would do something like that for Anyi," sighed Lihan, "it would make things so much easier."

A couple of days later, Anyi's father came to discuss the adoption of Imang. Ding marvelled as he watched his father talking with him. He was composed and relaxed, as he politely, but firmly, refused the witch-doctor's request.

"Yes," he said to the witch-doctor, "I know the consequences of ignoring dreams and of angering the spirits, but we are not following the spirits now—we are following the Lord Jesus."

The witch-doctor was scornful and his threats were hardly veiled, but realising that he was making no impression, he took his leave.

"Do you think he will come again?" Ding asked his father.

"Not before he has called on the spirits to help him," replied his father. "He will try every means to have his own way."

It was the next day that Imang fell. He and some of the other youngsters had been climbing up and down the verandah rails. Imang had fallen, striking his head on a notched pole as he did so.

Ding, coming in from the rice hut, saw a crowd gathering around the door of his room. Fear hastened his footsteps along the verandah. Pushing through the crowd he came to the little circle where Imang lay in his mother's arms. The little boy was deathly white and his breathing laboured. Ding knelt beside him. "Imang, Imang," he called softly, but Imang lay still and unresponsive.

In the background someone started the death wail. "Stop that," one of the older men called out sharply, "we are Christians now, we don't do that."

"What do we do?" asked someone.

"How do you bury him in this custom?" asked another.

"He's not dead yet."

"Huh! It won't be long."

A hubbub of voices arose as one and another recalled others who had had falls of this nature, and died. It was not intentional callousness. It was the realistic way they had of discussing such things.

Ding and Mujan sat close to their mother as some of the crowd drifted away. Someone had gone to the farm to call their father.

As the crowd thinned out, Ding saw Anyi standing, watching triumphantly. He didn't speak when Ding looked up, and having seen him, Ding did not look his way again.

"Hadn't we better call a witch-doctor?" The speaker was Ding's cousin.

"We are Christians—we do not follow the spirits." It was the first time Ding's mother had spoken.

"All very well, but the boy's nearly dead."

Ding's father came breathlessly into the room at this point. He was nearly as white as his little son, as he knelt beside him.

"What can we do?" Ding asked his father desperately.

The older man put his head between his hands. "I don't know, Ding. I think we must pray and ask the Lord Jesus to help us."

"He doesn't look as though he will be with us much longer." They looked up to see Anyi's father standing there: "What are you doing for him?"

"We are going to pray and ask the Lord Jesus to help him," replied Ding's father.

The witch-doctor's lips curled. "This is an expression of the spirits' anger," he said, "you had better ask them to help you."

Ding's father stood up and faced the witch-doctor squarely. "If this is from the spirits," he said quietly, "we have nothing to fear. The Lord Jesus is greater than the spirits; He will heal Imang."

"We will see who is the stronger," said the witch-doctor curtly, and turned on his heel and left them.

As he left the room, a sense of expectancy fell upon them. The atmosphere became oppressive and Ding felt the hair rising on the back of his neck. Imang began to toss restlessly; his breathing became more laboured.

A few minutes later Lihan came in. "The witch-doctor

is outside your door calling on the spirits," he whispered, his eyes wide with fear. They all knew the spirits were already in the room.

"Do something to appease the spirits quickly," cried Ding's uncle, "the boy is dying."

Ding saw his father look across at his mother. Her eyes were on their son. His condition was deteriorating rapidly.

Ding's father closed his eyes. "We will pray," he said firmly. "O great God of all the earth, our Father," he began, "in the Name of your Son, our Lord Jesus, we come to ask your help." At the mention of the Name of Jesus the oppressive atmosphere eased; Imang became still. Encouraged, his father continued, "Our little boy Imang is very ill. We believe he is ill because of the evil spirits. We ask you to heal him in the Name of Jesus. Amen."

Ding opened his eyes. The room was quiet. There was an atmosphere of peace such as he had never known before. He looked at Imang. He was breathing normally and the colour was returning to his face.

No one spoke. Even Ding's unbelieving uncle was awe-struck by what he was witnessing.

Imang's eyes opened. He yawned. "I'm hungry," he said.

Outside the door the witch-doctor was sitting in silence, stunned. Anyi, used to his father speaking with the spirits, realised something was different. He was sure his father was out of his trance and yet he seemed speechless. Anyi leaned forward and touched him. "Is anything wrong?" he asked anxiously.

Only the witch-doctor's lips moved as he replied: "The spirits said they have no power against the Name of Jesus."

Later, he was to bluster and make excuses and find ways through the spirits to make trouble in the long-house, but for the moment, stunned by the failure of the spirits against the power of Jesus, he spoke the truth.

It was late afternoon and Ding and Lihan sat on a rock overlooking the river. High in the sky flew a red hawk. Ding pointed it out to Lihan, and together they watched it swoop, and soar and circle.

Watching it, Ding felt a sense of elation and freedom. "Oh Lihan!" he exclaimed, "we are free to watch the red hawk, free to go to our farms no matter what birds cross our path, free to walk day or night without fear of the spirits. I hope we shall soon know more about the Lord Jesus, Who set us free."

14

"DING, how long is soon?" Ding looked up from mending his net. "What do you mean, Imang?" he asked.

"How long is soon?" Imang asked impatiently, tugging at the thin strip of hair hanging down his back.

Ding shrugged. "Soon means it won't be long. Why do you ask?"

"Because I heard our father say the missionary would be here soon," replied Imang.

"That means 'not very long'," Ding informed him.

"Do you think he will be here this afternoon?" Imang jumped up and down excitedly.

Ding's face clouded. "Not that soon," he replied.

"Tomorrow then?" squealed Imang.

"No, not tomorrow." Ding hated squashing the boy's enthusiasm.

Imang came to a halt. "But you said soon meant 'not very long'."

"Who said the missionary was coming soon?" Ding asked.

"I heard our father telling Anyi's father," pouted Imang, realising Ding wasn't really answering his question.

"Anyi's father?" Ding frowned.

"Yes, and Anyi's father just laughed, and"—Imang's eyes grew large, "he said we are like men in a canoe who have no pilot."

Imang spoke slowly, repeating something he had not understood. "What did he mean, Ding?"

Ding tugged at his strip of hair and wound it up into a tight knob at the back of his head.

"Anyi's father speaks in parables," he said evasively. He knew what the witch-doctor meant, but he did not want to explain it to Imang.

Before Imang could ask any further questions, another boy of Ding's age joined them. Ding was glad to see his friend Lihan.

"Where are you going, Lihan?" Ding asked the obvious.

"Fishing," replied Lihan, indicating the fishing net in one hand and a paddle in the other.

Ding was about to point out that it was a poor time for fishing, but noting the gloomy look on Lihan's face, he changed his mind. "Wait and I'll come too."

He was back in a few minutes, paddle in hand. Imang had wandered off. The boys walked in silence down to the river. Here they stepped into one of the canoes nudging the river bank and paddled out into midstream. No word had been spoken. Ding for his part was still thinking of what the witchdoctor had said.

"That parable has the sting of a scorpion," he thought and wriggled uncomfortably as though he actually felt the sting. In a way he did. There was truth in what the witch-doctor said.

A harvest had come and gone since the long-house at Long Nanga had decided to follow the way of Jesus. The year had been full of uncertainties for there was so much they didn't know. They wanted to ask so many questions and always there was the sneer of the witch-doctor: "Where is the missionary? Who is this Jesus we are following?"

It was true that Jesus was with them, but they knew so little about Him. The missionary had said that God's Book helped him to know Jesus and showed him what to do and say.

"We don't have God's Book. How are we to know if no one tells us?" thought Ding.

A grunt from Lihan brought him out of his reverie. They were at the foot of a rapid. Lihan laid down his paddle and reached for his pole. Ding did the same.

Ding and Lihan dug their poles into the rocky river bed.

Ding loved this fight against the forces of the river. It gave him a sense of power as inch by inch they moved up the river against all its attempts to send them hurtling back.

With a final heave they flung the canoe over the lip of the rapids. Quickly downing their poles they began paddling away from the draw of the rapid.

"Where are you going?" Ding asked of Lihan. He had expected to stop in the calm waters above the rapid, but it was obvious that Lihan intended to go on.

"Above Nahah Durian," answered Lihan.

"That's a long way!" exclaimed Ding.

Lihan shrugged. "There are often fish there when they are nowhere else," he replied. "I can't come back empty handed."

"So that's it," thought Ding. "That's why Lihan looks so gloomy and paddles with a tense hunch to his shoulders. Urei has been complaining that he is a poor provider."

Ding was right. Anger welled up inside Lihan as he remembered the sneering taunts of his wife. What did she expect? Fish were scarce—so were wild pig. It wasn't as if he hadn't been trying. He had been out several nights hunting pig. He was tired. A while ago he had lain down on the mat for a sleep. Immediately Urei had started her nagging. "He was lazy! She was hungry. Didn't he care about their child soon to be born . . ." and so on! Wearily he had got to his feet and left the room. Her shrill voice still rang in his ears.

"Poor Lihan," thought Ding. He could tell by the way Lihan was paddling that his thoughts were angry ones.

Lihan had not wanted to marry Urei. His parents had arranged the marriage. Lihan's mother was not very strong and needed a daughter-in-law to help her, and she had been watching Urei for some time. She was industrious and not afraid of hard work.

Lihan had viewed her differently. She was not good looking, and the lobes of her ears, instead of stretching gracefully as heavy rings were added, had stretched into lumpy strings. One ear-lobe had finally broken. Her slant eyes darted hither and thither missing nothing. She seemed to have a perpetual sneer and he knew her reputation for a bad temper. He had told his parents he did not want to marry her, but he had been afraid to say that it was Ding's sister he wanted. They weren't listening anyway, as they were too busy working out the details of his marriage to Urei.

Thud! The boys looked in the direction of the noise and without a word changed course for the near river bank.

Lihan leapt out before the canoe had touched the shore and disappeared into the undergrowth. He came back smiling broadly. He was holding the stalk of a large round fruit with sharp spikes. "That's Anyi's tree," he grinned, pointing with his chin toward the durian tree which towered above the undergrowth.

They both laughed. To climb a tree and pick fruit would be stealing, but if you happened to find fruit that had fallen to the ground it was yours.

Lihan drew his malit (long jungle knife) from its sheath and was about to open the durian when his face clouded. He paused and looked at Ding. Ding sighed. He understood. Lihan was thinking that if they didn't catch any fish perhaps this delicious fruit would appease his wife somewhat.

"Come on," said Ding and prepared to paddle off. Lihan laid the durian carefully in the bottom of the canoe and picked up his paddle. The sweet smell of the durian drifted to Ding as they paddled, and his mouth watered.

"Did you hear what Imang was saying when you came along?" he asked by way of taking his mind off the durian and Lihan's mind off his troubles.

"No I didn't hear," replied Lihan disinterestedly.

Ding told him. Lihan frowned.

"Anyi's father is always saying things like that," he said. "But lately he has been hinting at something more."

"What do you mean?" Ding asked.

"I don't really know." Lihan gave his hair a tug. "He has some scheme I'm sure. I just don't know what it is."

15

"Look who's coming." Ding spoke softly. Lihan nodded. He had already seen Anyi and his brother Jau paddling toward them.

Ding and Lihan prepared to ignore the two boys, but Anyi and Jau paddled close to them. Anyi saw the durian and his eyes narrowed. His family owned all the durian trees on that stretch of bank. "Where did you get that?"

Ding smiled mischievously. He didn't hate Anyi any more, but he enjoyed teasing him. "On the ground," he said. "We heard it fall."

"That's off our tree," said Anyi angrily.

"Your tree, is it?" said Ding innocently. "Well it should be nice."

Anyi and his brother had almost passed them and Anyi was about to retort when a sneer spread over his sullen features. "Keep it for your missionary," he taunted. Whereupon he and his brother laughed maliciously and sped on their way.

Ding and Lihan pretended not to hear, but inwardly they squirmed.

"Why doesn't he come?" exclaimed Lihan when the boys were out of sight. "No wonder they taunt us. We are like fatherless children."

Ding did not reply. The fact that the missionary hadn't returned was like an ache inside him. He knew many in the longhouse were also disappointed. A few had even gone back to buying a charm or two secretly just to make sure that they would be "safe".

Anyi's father, although he had taken the name of Christian with everyone else, had only thrown out a few useless charms. He was still practising witchcraft and trying to draw others in the long-house back to old beliefs.

Still, although no one understood very much, the majority clung tenaciously to the fact that Jesus had delivered them from the power of the evil spirits. Only a few heeded the witch-doctor.

They were just below Nahah Durian now and Lihan called a halt. While Ding kept the canoe steady he threw the net high into the air. It came down like a giant spider web onto the surface of the water, then the heavy rings encircling it drew it below. Lihan waited a few minutes before commencing to pull in the string attached to the middle of the net. The net was empty. Again and again he cast it, but each time it was empty. Not even a small fish!

At last he gave an exclamation of disgust. "It's no use," he said, throwing the net to the bottom of the canoe and taking up his paddle. "Let her nag," he muttered, thinking of his disgruntled wife.

He indicated to Ding that they should pull into the river bank. As the canoe touched shore Lihan laid down his paddle, picked up the durian and leapt ashore. He drew out his malit and started to open the prickly fruit. "Come on, Ding, let's enjoy it. Why should I give it to Urei?"

Ding was amazed at his friend's behaviour. It was so unlike Lihan. He tied the canoe to a stump and sat down on a log. Having split the fruit open with his malit, Lihan proceeded gingerly to break the rest of it open, exposing the delicious creamy flesh in its pods. He handed some to Ding.

Ding smacked his lips and dug a piece of fruit out of the pods with his fingers. It tasted delicious. He sucked a huge piece till only the seed remained and then dug into another pod for more.

It was finished too soon. "I wish we had some more," said Lihan.

They washed their hands and faces and set off downriver again.

For all his bravado Ding knew he wasn't looking forward to going home empty-handed. Marriage had certainly changed Lihan. "Let's try the net again just before the next rapid," he suggested.

Lihan gave a non-committal grunt. As they paddled downstream Ding's thoughts went to the missionary again. If only he were here he would know how to help Lihan. There would be something in that Book to help. Suddenly Ding sat up. The help Lihan wanted right now was fish. What if they were to ask the Lord Jesus?

They had asked Him to help when Imang was nearly dead and Imang had been healed. They had prayed for a good harvest and their harvest had been the best they could remember. Other times of asking help came to his mind. But this was just a little thing. Would the Lord Jesus answer?

They had reached the calm waters above Batu Aru. "Lihan, let's ask the Lord Jesus to help us catch some fish," suggested Ding.

"He wouldn't be interested in helping us do something like that," said Lihan half-heartedly. "Let's ask Him," said Ding.

"All right. You ask Him."

They bowed their heads and Ding prayed simply. "Lord Jesus, we don't know if you are interested in catching fish, but you know the trouble Lihan is having with Urei. Please help him to catch some fish. We ask in your Name. Amen."

Eagerly Ding watched Lihan poise himself on the prow of the canoe and cast the net. As Lihan began to draw it in, it was obvious that it was empty. Lihan looked at Ding. "Try again, Lihan." Ding felt sure that their prayer would be answered. The net was cast again.

"Yes." Lihan dived over the side and into the water. He came up spluttering and threw a good-sized fish into the canoe. Next time he came up with two smaller ones and climbed back in. His eyes were shining. "The Lord Jesus really must have heard us!" He cast the net again and caught two more fish. After that, although he cast several times, there were no more.

"It is enough, Lihan," said Ding. "We asked the Lord Jesus to help us and He did. He gave us enough."

Now as they continued down-river there was a new rhythm to Lihan's paddling. He whooped in anticipation as they prepared to negotiate the swirling midstream of the rapids. Arriving at the riverside, Lihan started to divide the fish, but Ding picked up one of the bigger fish. "This will do," he said and meandered off.

Lihan entered his room and threw the fish indifferently beside the fire where his unhappy wife was cooking rice. "About time," was all she said. His mother-in-law looked up from her matmaking in a corner of the room and sniffed. Lihan went into the *tilung* (tiny sleeping and cooking room) and lay down on the mat. Perhaps now he could have a sleep. "Another harvest and I will be out of this room," he thought.

It was Kayan custom for the bridegroom to live in the room of his bride, but other arrangements could be made. Their parents had arranged that he would live in Urei's room until the second harvest after their marriage and after that the couple would move to Lihan's room permanently. Lihan's mother had wanted the couple to come straight away. However Urei's mother was adamant that the couple should spend two harvests with her.

Lihan was almost asleep when the shrill voice of his wife reached him.

"There are those who think we women can cook fish without wood," came the whining voice. "We women are clever, but who heard of a woman cooking without wood."

Lihan gritted his teeth as he got up. So she wanted firewood, did she? Where was Urei's older brother? He was a provider for the room too. Taking his malit from where it hung on the deer antlers, he stumped out of the room.

He almost bumped into Ding on the verandah. Ding did not notice his friend's agitation. "Sit down," he said indicating a spot on the long-house verandah. They sat down and Ding looked around to make sure no one was listening.

"Lihan, what does 'Bungan' mean?"

"Bungan?" repeated Lihan. "I don't know. Where did you hear it?" "I was passing Anyi's father. He was talking with a couple of other men and I heard the witchdoctor say: 'I tell you 'Bungan' is the answer.' Just then Anyi saw me and gave one of those horrible sneers."

Ding paused and cracked the knuckles of his hands one by one, then continued. "I don't know what it means. I feel it has something to do with following the Lord Jesus and the fact that Anyi's father doesn't want us to."

"Maybe 'Bungan' is someone we could follow." Ding was shocked at Lihan's words. "But we follow the Lord Jesus. We don't want to follow anyone else," he exclaimed.

"We follow in a way," said Lihan slowly, "but we don't really know about Him."

"The missionary will teach us when he comes," replied Ding. Then seeing the sarcastic look on his friend's face, he hurriedly added, "and we do know the Lord Jesus answers prayer."

The sarcastic look vanished from Lihan's face. In his anger against Urei he had forgotten the way the Lord Jesus had answered their prayer for fish

He looked thoughtfully at his friend. "Yes, the Lord Jesus did answer our prayer," he said slowly, "but" he frowned, "there are lots of things we don't know and it doesn't look as though the missionary is coming back. I guess he doesn't really care about us."

Ding felt the ache inside him that often came when he thought of the missionary. "Maybe Anyi's father knows a better way," Lihan continued.

16

"WHAT do you mean?" Ding was almost angry. It was Lihan's turn to crack his knuckle joints. "Well, we haven't got anyone to help us or teach us. In our old custom we knew what to do, but I don't know what to do about Urei. I hate her. I don't want her."

Ding was stunned. He didn't know what to say. "You will settle down, Lihan," he said lamely. "You know it takes time to settle down. Remember Paya' Ngau and Juk La'ing. It was five years before they became used to one another."

This was cold comfort to Lihan. "I couldn't put up with her for five years," he said. "The old people keep saying we will get used to one another. But I don't want to get used to her." "Then there is the baby," said Ding vaguely. He felt that might help, somehow.

Lihan's face softened. "Yes, there's the baby," he repeated. "You know, when the baby is born I would like to take it and go back to my own room and leave Urei where she is."

"You can't do that!" Ding exclaimed.

"You don't understand, Ding."

They sat in silence. Ding felt sorry for Lihan. He was thankful that his parents had chosen Usun for him. When they married he knew that they would at least like one another. He was sure they would soon get used to one another's ways. He was more disturbed about Lihan listening to the witch-doctor than he was about his attitude to Urei.

He wondered what the missionary would do if he were here. Then he remembered how he had once hated Anyi.

He had asked God to change him and help him to like Anyi instead. God had done it!

If he could like Anyi surely Lihan could love Urei. Come to think of it, if Lihan loved Urei he would be less likely to listen to the witch-doctor.

Ding started to crack his knuckles again. "Remember how I used to hate Anyi?" he asked Lihan.

"Yes," said Lihan, "but this is different."

"The missionary made me see I wasn't so wonderful either," Ding went on.

Lihan looked at him in disgust. "You don't understand," he repeated and stood up. "I am going to get some wood." Ding did not offer to go with him. He felt miserable. He didn't know how to help his friend.

"What is 'Bungan,' Ding?" Startled, Ding found Imang beside him.

"What do you know about 'Bungan'?" he asked abruptly.

"I don't know anything. What is it?" insisted the little boy.

"Where did you hear about it?" Ding asked.

"That horrible Anyi just pulled my hair and said, 'Bungan is the one my little boy, Bungan is the one'. I'm not his little boy, anyway." he added vehemently.

"Bungan is the one," Ding repeated slowly. Bungan must be a person then, or, Ding hesitated to even think about it, "Could Bungan be another god? The missionary said there was only one God. No, 'Bungan' couldn't be another god." He sat for a while thinking about Lihan and Bungan. Then he got up and pulled at his hair impatiently. He wished he knew what it was all about.

He was about to go into his room when someone came hurrying along the verandah and as he came closer Ding recognised Lihan's brother-in-law. "Have you seen Lihan?" he asked. "He went out to get some wood," replied Ding. "Do you know where he went?"

85

"Not really," said Ding, although he had a fair idea. "Why do you want him?"

"His wife needs him."

Instantly Ding understood. Urei was going to have her baby. "I will go and look for him if you like," he said.

"Go, and go quickly." The man turned and hurried back down the verandah.

Ding knew there were two places that Lihan liked to go for wood. He reasoned he would go to the nearest as he was alone and he was right. He could hear Lihan chopping before he reached him.

Lihan looked around when he heard Ding.

"Urei needs you," Ding told him. Lihan swept the perspiration from his face, sheathed his malit and set off with Ding. He did not stop to collect the little wood he had cut.

Ding knew it was not from concern for Urei that he came quickly, but rather because it was the right thing to do. He was about to be a father and he did not want to lose face before the people of the long-house.

17

DING, Mujan his sister and their parents sat eating the evening meal. Imang was wandering around with a leaf-full of rice, nibbling as he went.

Ding was thinking about Lihan and wondering if the baby was born. It was strange to think of Lihan as a father. They had been boys together, fought and played, fished and hunted together. Now things were different. He had noticed it when Lihan first married. He was no longer free to come and go with Ding as he pleased. He had changed in other ways too.

"We will go and see the farm tomorrow." His father broke into his thoughts. "It should be time for weeding."

"The chief's room has started," said Mujan.

Ding got up, his parcel of rice half eaten. He picked it up and pushed it down a hole in the floor. There was a quick response from the pigs below. His mother noticed how concerned he was for his friend and gently chided him. "Let Lihan worry. You should eat."

Ding picked up his home-made guitar. "I'm going for a walk," he said.

Strolling down the long-house verandah, Ding strummed on the guitar and was soon joined by some of his friends attracted by the monotonous, but strangely haunting music. They wandered to the end of the verandah and turned back.

"Anyone heard any news?" asked Ding.

"No," replied one boy. "The old ones are there, and Lihan, but there is no news."

"Who is Bungan?" asked Ding as they continued their strolling. Another boy had joined them with his guitar.

"Who is Bungan?" repeated some of the boys. "I don't know," said one, "but it has something to do with someone down-river whom Anyi's father met."

"Is Bungan a person?"

"Who knows? Perhaps so, perhaps not."

No one knew any more than that. The group came to a room where some of the girls were sitting.

The girls appeared to be oblivious of them but the titters and giggles that burst out from time to time told a different story. The boys pretended to ignore the girls but made no attempt to go through the little door into the next room.

A head popped out from a tilung. "Come on there, dance!" It was the father of one of the boys. Slowly they spread out and sat down, meanwhile urging one of their number to dance.

With a wild shriek and a stamp of his foot a boy jumped into the circle and started to dance the dance of the jungle-vine gatherer. It was a gleeful dance and the boy did it well, but already the boys were calling Ding to do the dance of the head-hunter.

The first boy ended his dance. Another boy came up to Ding with a sheathed malit, another with a shield. From within the tilung came a shuffling sound and a leopard skin and feather headband were tossed out.

Reluctantly—he would be thought proud if he appeared eager—Ding handed his guitar to another boy and took the things offered to him.

Dressed in his regalia, arms swinging loosely beside him, he swayed toward the middle of the floor. Eyes uplifted, face solemn, he seemed oblivious to everyone in the room.

But he wasn't. He was wide awake to Usun sitting back in the shadows. He had never been so conscious of her before. He wanted to dance for her and her alone. He suddenly realised it was time he got on with the dance.

He gave an earpiercing shriek. The girls jumped and

screamed and giggled even though they had been expecting it. When Ding started the graceful, intricate dance,
everyone was silent. The silence pleased Ding. It was a
tribute to his ability.

A wild flourish of his malit and a shriek of victory
brought him to the end of the dance. He shot a glance at
Usun for her approval. She didn't seem to have noticed.
With a shock Ding realised it wasn't the pretended cool-
ness that was a normal part of tribal courtship. Something
told him there was a coldness there and that was unlike
Usun.

"A girl! A girl! Let a girl dance!" The boys were
taking up the call of the man sitting in the tilung. The
girls were tittering and nudging one another.

With forced gaiety Ding pranced in front of the girls.
He pretended to try and drag first this one and then that
one into the centre. Finally he reached for Usun as everyone knew he would. She resisted his pulling and he felt it
wasn't the resistance of custom, but finally she came out,
pushed by the girls and pulled by Ding.

Fitting gloves of feathers on her fingers she started to
dance the slow and graceful dance of the birds. Ding
couldn't take his eyes off her. Desire welled up in him.
He must tell his parents he was ready for marriage. Even
as he thought this he was conscious that there was something lacking in her dancing. She wasn't dancing for him.
It was as if he wasn't there.

What was wrong? Ding searched in his mind. Perhaps
he had offended her. Usun's parents didn't seem to have
entered wholeheartedly into the Christian faith like some.
Still, relations between their parents were good and both
parents favoured the marriage.

She was considered to be a long-house beauty. Her ear-
lobes were weighted with a mass of brass rings and stretched
below her shoulders. Her skin was smooth and unblem-
ished. Through the gossip channels he knew her to be good

tempered and hard working. What more could he ask for?

Suddenly he sensed a change. It was as though she was really coming alive. His pulse quickened. It was all right after all; this was the way she always danced for him.

Then an uneasiness descended upon him. Slowly, almost involuntarily, he turned his head until he found himself looking up into the face of Anyi. Anyi had just come into the room and was still standing. Usun's dancing had changed when he came in. Ding knew. He knew by the triumphant look on his face that Anyi knew it too.

18

THE baby was not born when Ding went to bed, but his concern for Lihan was almost totally eclipsed by Usun's attitude to him and Anyi's obvious triumph. He knew she had always been indifferent to Anyi. She may even have disliked him. Why should she change? "Well she cannot marry him," thought Ding, "we are promised to one another." It was cold comfort and he slept restlessly.

Chinks of light were showing through the wall of the rough-hewn boards in Ding's room. When he awoke he was conscious of loud whispering.

"Then what does Jesus do?" He recognised one of his mother's friends. What was she doing here at this time of the morning?

"I don't know," he heard his mother say, "but that is old custom."

The other woman snorted. "That's all you can say— 'That is old custom'," she mimicked. "What's Jesus' custom, that's what I want to know."

Mujan told him, "Urei's baby had a strange birth."

"Strange?" exclaimed Ding in dismay.

Mujan moved over close to Ding. "They want to let it die."

Ding cracked his knuckle joints tensely. If a baby was not born in the normal way it was a bad omen.

"What is the omen?" he asked Mujan.

"If it is allowed to live it will grow up and kill somebody," Mujan informed him.

"That was old custom." Ding voiced his thoughts to Mujan.

"Yes," she replied dolefully, "but what is the Jesus way?"

Ding tried to think of something the missionary had said that would help. He could think of nothing.

"I think Urei's mother wants to let it die," Mujan went on. "But Lihan's mother isn't so sure. She said it was old custom so it couldn't be right. What do you think, Ding?"

Ding wished she wouldn't ask him. "Let's go down there," he said.

They found the room crowded. A new baby always created interest.

Everyone was talking in loud whispers one to the other.

Suddenly a strong cry silenced the crowd.

"He is strong."

"They should have stuffed its mouth with salt. It would be dead now," rasped one old crone.

A murmur of voices arose and discussion began once more.

"Are they going to let it die?"

"That's old custom."

"Well, what is new custom?"

"What does the Jesus way do about this?"

"The missionary didn't say. Why didn't he tell us?"

"Why doesn't he come back and tell us?"

"I say let it die. We don't know what Jesus does."

"That's right. And it's just a nameless thing."

"I don't know about that. It's old custom."

"Well what is new custom?"

The discussion went round and round in circles. There seemed to be no solution. Lihan wasn't taking part in it but sat leaning up against the wall of the tilung looking tired and worn. Lihan's family and Urei's family talked quietly together.

There was a stir. Anyi's father entered and took a prominent place in the room. Ding remembered that he was a relative of Urei's mother. He would have a say whether he was asked or not.

"Well, what is to be done?" He looked at Urei's father and Lihan's father, and at the two mothers. Then he looked at Lihan and slowly gazed around the room. "What does Jesus say about this?" His gaze came to rest on Ding's father. Ding felt sorry for his father. He was always called on in these matters concerning the new way. He could remember much of what the missionary said, but even so he knew very little.

"What shall we do?" Ding's father echoed the question. "This is a new thing."

"There are many new things." The witch-doctor's words were polite. "But we do not know them. Where is our missionary father? Can a child grow without his father?"

Ding felt like answering cheekily, "Yes a child can," but he knew, as did everyone present, exactly what the witch-doctor was saying.

"It is true, we are like fatherless children," Ding's father spoke up. "We have no one to tell us more of this way. However it would seem from what we know of the Jesus way that we should keep this nameless one."

Ding knew it was a weak argument. He agreed with his father, but he knew that the people would want something definite. They needed someone who could say, "When we follow the Lord Jesus, we do this or that."

"Of course you are right, brother," replied the witch-doctor, smoothly. "We really know so little of the Jesus way, it is hard to know what seems good or bad."

Ding noted that the witch-doctor had not referred to custom at all. "He is a sly one," he thought to himself.

Everyone had quietened down to listen to the witch-doctor. Now a murmur of voices began again.

"That's right. It is only a nameless thing."

"Didn't the missionary say they gave their babies names

when they were born? Could that be the custom?"

"Perhaps, but this is still a nameless one. And it was born strangely. Surely the Lord Jesus wouldn't expect us to keep a baby born strangely."

"The spirits might be angry too." Several people frowned at the speaker who had dared to voice the thoughts of some.

"We are not following the spirits," someone reprimanded him.

"At least we would know what to do if we were," grumbled another.

"You young ones wouldn't remember Kalang Imang," remarked the witch-doctor. Everyone became silent again, the older ones because they did remember, the others because they sensed a story.

Inwardly pleased at the attention he had gained, the witch-doctor looked solemn.

"I was not walking when he was born," he went on. "He was born strangely and had this same omen, but no one knew at the time." He paused to let the last statement sink in. "His grandmother was the only one who knew. She helped with his delivery." Again he paused, letting his cunning eyes sweep over his listeners. "She wanted a grandson. Her own three children were girls. So far her daughters had also given birth to girls. She longed for a grandson, so she hid the facts of his birth." The witch-doctor laughed mirthlessly. "As if you could hide anything from the evil spirits."

Ding shivered. There was something ominous about the way the witch-doctor said those last words.

"When he was of age (a baby did not have a name until it was a year old) he was given the name of Wan. However he was a naughty child and had much sickness. No doubt the evil spirits were angry. They gave plenty of warning that he was not a favoured child.

"Foolish grandmother, for now she had another grandson and this first one didn't really matter. But she was stubborn," (he shot a glance at Lihan), "and frightened" (his eyes rested on Lihan's mother), "and she wouldn't tell." He continued, "This child Wan became very ill. It looked as though he would die. Still the grandmother clung to him. Witch-doctors were called. His name was changed to Kalang to fool the evil spirits. He got better and the grandmother thought he was safe from the consequences of the omen too. Bah! Foolish woman!" ejaculated the witchdoctor.

"We were all at the marrying age when it happened. Of course we didn't know about the omen and Kalang was just one of us. He was rather bad tempered and not very popular."

"One day we were swimming in the river. Kalang's younger brother, the only other boy in the family, was teasing him. When they reached the shore Kalang picked up a piece of wood and struck his brother hard." Again the witchdoctor paused for effect. "He killed him." There was a gasp all round. "The men rushed to hold him but he dived into the water and swam to the other side of the river. Some of the men followed him into the jungle, but they didn't find him."

"What happened to him?" someone asked.

The witchdoctor eyed the questioner thoughtfully. "That was the strange thing. We never found out." Again a gasp swept the room. There was always something uncanny about a person who just disappeared.

"You never found the body?" a youth asked.

"No never," replied the witch-doctor.

"And the grandmother?"

"Ah, yes. The grandmother, foolish woman! Only then did she tell us the truth about his birth. Then she went out into the jungle and chewed some poisonous leaves. She too died." There was an oppressive silence. The witch-doctor had made his point and there was none to say: "But Jesus said . . ."

Ding wandered back to his room. He felt a great heaviness upon him. The ultimate decision lay with the two families, but he felt they would be influenced by the witch-doctor. Mujan came in. "What do you think will happen, Ding?"

"I don't know," Ding replied slowly. He would like to have talked to Lihan. He wondered how he felt about it all. He had tried to catch Lihan's eye but his friend had seemed oblivious to everyone in the room.

Ding's father came into the room. Ding didn't have to ask what had been decided. He could tell by his father's face that the baby was to die.

His father pushed a board aside in the wall and the sunlight streamed in. He stood there looking out.

"The clever-tongued one is still powerful," he said of the witch-doctor. "The missionary must come soon and teach us. The witch-doctor is right—we are like fatherless children."

"They are going to let it die." There were tears in Mujan's eyes.

Her father turned abruptly. "Let us go to the farm."

"There is wisdom in this," thought Ding. In old custom they would not have dared to leave the house until the baby was dead and the witch-doctor had sanctioned their going.

"I'll meet you at the river," said Ding. He wanted to see his friend. The crowd had thinned out in the room and Ding went and sat near Lihan. Lihan had not moved.

"It has been decided?" Ding did not look at his friend as he spoke.

It seemed like an age before Lihan answered.

"It has been decided," his voice was barely audible. Instinctively Ding knew his friend was against the decision. From inside the tilung came the sound of weeping. Perhaps Urei was too. But the old people were the ones who had made the decision.

Ding longed to say something to comfort his friend, but all he said was, "We are going to the farm." As he spoke a strong cry came from the other side of the room. Ding looked up, startled. Then he realised it was the baby, put there in the corner, to be neglected till it died. His eyes met Lihan's and for a moment he saw the depth of anguish there. From inside the tilung came a convulsive sob. The crying continued. The atmosphere was oppressive.

"I'm going," said Ding, glad to leave but hating himself for not staying. Lihan gave no sign that he had heard.

Ding walked slowly to the river. Suddenly he felt angry. Why didn't the missionary come? Why did he leave them to follow blindly? If he were here to teach them they would know what to do.

He shook his head as if trying to shake the cry of the baby and the angry thought about the missionary from his head. He hoped the baby would be dead by the time he got back. He didn't want to hear it cry again.

19

DING could hear the baby crying weakly when they returned from the farm that evening. He wanted to put his hands over his ears and blot out the noise. For the sake of his friend he forced himself to go to the room. Lihan was not in the family room. His mother was sitting there. Ding tried not to look at the corner where the baby lay crying feebly. He looked at Lihan's mother. "How can you bear it, mother?" (mother was a term of respect).

"It must be this way," she replied. "We do not know any other way."

"I cannot believe this is the Way of the Lord Jesus," said Ding.

"Maybe it isn't, child," she spoke gently, "but we do not know the way of the Lord Jesus yet. The witch-doctor felt this was best."

"So," thought Ding, "she isn't really happy about it."

There was movement from within the tilung and Lihan came out. He sat on the floor and leaned against the wall. He did not look at Ding.

Ding walked over and sat close to him. The baby had stopped its crying and was whimpering. Ding gritted his teeth. For Lihan's sake he must stay awhile.

He glanced at Lihan and saw something of the torment through which his friend was going. He wanted to say something to help and comfort.

"It is hard," was all he said.

"It is hard," repeated Lihan.

"The old people say this is best," said Ding.

"The old people say this is best," repeated Lihan.

"If only we knew what the Lord Jesus would do." Ding tugged his hair.

"Do not torture yourselves, it is a nameless thing," said Lihan's mother.

"But it cries," said Ding. "It lives."

"It is nothing. Do not think about it." Urei's mother came out of the tilung and joined them.

"It is something, mother," said Ding, angrily. "Can't you hear it? Do you not care?"

Urei's mother glared at him. "Listen to the stripling talk. Do you not care?" she mimicked. "What do you know about caring? What do you know about longing to go and pick up the nameless thing and feed it and fondle it? What do you know of the pain of a mother as she listens?"

Ding was silent before her outburst. So the old people did feel it.

"I remember the nameless thing I had. I was Urei's age," she reminisced. "A beautiful nameless thing. It was my first. His body was fat and healthy. His cry was strong and lusty. But," she paused and Ding felt more than saw, the tears in her eyes, "his foot was twisted. How could he have walked? He could never have come to the farm with us or fought the mighty river; fished and hunted like others. It was a bad omen. So we put him in the corner where that nameless one is now. He cried. Oh, how he cried. Finally we stuffed his mouth with salt. He died quickly then."

"That was the way of the evil spirits, Mother." Ding wanted to plead for the life of his friend's baby, but she glared at him again. "And what is the way of this Jesus?" she asked. "We should never have listened to that missionary. Then we would have known this was the way. We would not have hoped there was another way. We would have accepted this agony for what it is."

The feeble cry started again. From within the tilung came the sound of heart-breaking sobs.

"Poor Urei," thought Ding. The feeble cry continued

on the other side of the room. Ding couldn't bear any more.

"I am going now," he said.

"Go well," murmured Lihan. The two women said nothing. Ding walked through the little doors between the rooms. Three rooms away he came to Usun's room. Occupied with his thoughts, trying to get away quickly from the pathetic cry, he hardly noticed he was in her room until he was half way across. Then he realised someone was strumming quietly on a guitar in the corner of the room. He knew without looking that it was Anyi. Usun was sitting on the platform with one of her friends. She did not look at him.

He continued on his way. Indignation and anger welled up within him. What were Usun's parents doing letting Anyi in there like that. It was Ding's right, as the one engaged to Usun, to visit her room at night, to play to her, to court her. Her parents should not allow Anyi to be there. He clenched his hands. What should he do?

"What is the matter my son?"

He had been so engrossed with his thoughts that he hadn't noticed his mother sitting there. He looked at her now. She sat close to the feeble resin lamp, the only light in the room and she was weaving a mat.

Ding cracked his knuckle joints one by one in rapid succession. "Are we of the same heart, mother?" he asked.

"The same heart?" his mother questioned.

"What about my friend?" Ding went on, "I would like to know about my friend."

"So it should be," agreed his mother. "I will talk to her mother." She did not enquire any further, presuming Ding's edginess to be that of a young man's desire.

Ding slept restlessly. His sleep was alive with dreams. They were a confused mixture of nameless things; Anyi, Usun, guitar-strumming and marriage. He was glad when morning came and they prepared to go to the farm to do the weeding. Before leaving, Ding called in to see Lihan.

There was no sound as Ding entered the room. Urei's mother put her head out of the tilung. "He is asleep," she informed Ding. "Let him sleep." Ding turned to go. Against his will he shot a glance at the corner where the baby had been. He couldn't see if it was still there. He took a step toward the door and then he heard it—a soft piteous sound from the corner. Ding fled from the room.

20

DING avoided looking at the place as they came home from weeding. It was two days since Lihan's baby had died and he knew that the body had been left in a tree. That was old custom for a baby without a name. No one knew what to do now. How long did one wait before naming a baby? If it died without a name what did one do? There had been much discussion, but no answers, so it had been buried in the same way as nameless babies of the past.

Stepping out of the canoe, Ding saw Lihan and Urei's family pulling into the shore a little further down-river. Lihan looked tired and gaunt. His mother-in-law was obviously giving him a tongue lashing about something and Ding could see by the set of his jaw that Lihan was angry.

Ding was about to go to his friend when he saw him pick up a bundle of wood and stalk off without a backward glance at his mother-in-law. He sighed.

"They're a sharp tongued family that lot," said his mother, who had been watching the scene too. "I told the mother of Lihan she was looking for trouble marrying into that family. She has plenty of it too."

"Lihan is the one who is getting all the trouble," replied Ding.

"It is certainly not easy for him," agreed his mother. "Still his parents are having their share of trouble. Urei's mother keeps demanding more sarongs and gifts for other members of the family as compensation for the fact that Lihan and Urei will not be staying in their room."

"They say that Lihan's family is to blame for the strange birth too." Mujan joined in.

"Of course they would blame his family," sniffed their mother. "That lot would never take the blame for anything." When he had eaten Ding went to Lihan's room. He hadn't seen him since the baby's death. He knew Urei had been very ill. She had followed the usual custom of women when they had a baby and had sat with her back to the fire. "The closer one sat, the quicker one became stronger," said the old midwives. Urei had sat very close and, like so many before her, her back had become badly blistered. The blisters had broken and become infected.

Urei's parents were in the room when Ding entered.

"Where is Lihan?" he asked.

"Where did he go, I wonder?" said Lihan's father-in-law.

"Through there," he pointed with his chin to the little door leading into the adjoining room. "But I don't know where he was going."

As they went on through the rooms Ding was puzzled. "Was Lihan on the verandah?" he wondered. They were almost to Anyi's room. He and Lihan rarely came to this end of the long-house.

The room next to Anyi's was empty and Ding guessed that the people were next door. They were related to the witch-doctor.

Ding and his friend peered through the chinks in the loosely tied boards which served as a partition between rooms.

At the far end of the room he could see the witch-doctor. He was sitting cross-legged and straight-backed on the mat. His eyes were alert and calculating. Ding shivered. There was something evil about the man. "Who would teach us?" Someone was asking. Ding did not recognise the speaker and tried to make out who it was through the other spaces between the planks of the wall. He didn't see the speaker, but he did see Lihan and others sitting back against the wall, listening.

Ding frowned. Lihan had always shared his feelings about the witch-doctor. He had never known him to enter Anyi's room voluntarily, let alone sit and join in a conversation with him.

Squinting through more of the cracks, he saw Anyi sitting a little way off from Lihan. His attention was not centred on his father.

Ding tried to see who Anyi was looking at. Whoever it was sat just out of Ding's sight, but he knew by the look on Anyi's face that it was Usun. Ding felt angry and bewildered. What had happened to Usun? What was she doing there? "There is not a lot to teach." Ding's attention was drawn back to Anyi's father. "I learned much when I was down-river," he said smoothly. "And there are those from the river Batang who would come and help us to get started." Ding's eyes narrowed. What was the witch-doctor talking about? The word Bungan flashed into his mind. Was he about to learn the meaning of Bungan?

One of the village elders was speaking: "We have made a choice. It would not be good to change again. We would be ashamed when the missionary comes back."

"Is he coming back?" There was a sneer in the witch-doctor's voice. "How wonderful is this Jesus that His messengers leave us like dogs without a master. If He was so powerful and important wouldn't we have had more teaching by now? Uh!"—he snorted his disgust.

Ding winced. "Who is Bungan?" asked Lihan. Ding glanced again at Lihan. It must have taken a lot of courage for him to speak.

"Bungan is the wife of God," said the witch-doctor looking straight at Lihan. "She made herself known to a man called Juk Apui in a dream."

Against his better judgment Ding found himself interested. "There are many spirits under her command," went on the witch-doctor. "But she is kind and the spirits will not harm us if we make the right sacrifices."

"Sacrifices!" exclaimed the committee man. "Must we go back to that again?"

"Ah, but these are only small sacrifices," explained the witch-doctor. "Not expensive things like pigs—just fowls and eggs."

"And there is none of this foolishness about not drinking borak," put in a man whom Ding knew to be Anyi's uncle.

"Mmmm" grunted the elder and Ding knew the speaker had made a point.

Borak (rice beer) had been a favourite drink. Feasting and drunkenness had been an inseparable part of Kayan life. However the missionary had warned that such behaviour was not pleasing to Jesus.

It was known that when the Kelabit and Murut tribesfolk had become Christian they had made a clean break. They had put away their beer-drinking and tobacco, vowing not to be ensnared again.

However the Kayan of Long Nanga had felt that that was rather drastic. "Let us keep a little," they said. "It will do no harm to have a little to drink." Unfortunately, after a couple of drinks many forgot that a little was enough and became drunk and quarrelsome.

Ding was thankful that his father had done with it altogether. He remembered the times his father had been violently ill-tempered through drinking. He remembered the fighting it had caused and the times as a little boy he had been hungry and uncared for while his parents were in a drunken stupor. He felt it was something they could well be rid of altogether.

"Is this Bungan, then, the mother of Jesus?" It was Lihan who asked the question that was in Ding's mind.

"Bungan is powerful," answered the witch-doctor. "Would she need a Son?" He paused. "No, I think not."

It wasn't so much what he said, but the way he said it that made Ding feel sick. He seemed to be dismissing Jesus as a mere nobody while Bungan became everything.

"These sacrifices—do we make them often?" The committee man appeared more interested now.

"That depends on many things," answered the witch-doctor evasively.

"It's just like our old custom," Lihan spoke up again. Ding was surprised as Lihan had always been diffident in the presence of the witch-doctor.

The witch-doctor eyed him thoughtfully. Ding had the feeling that he was planning an answer that would win Lihan over. He would anticipate all the doubts and questions in Lihan's mind.

"No, my son, it is not the same. The old spirits were hard task masters, but Bungan is good. Is she not God's wife?" "We cannot think about this lightly," said the committee man. "It is true we have no one to teach us, but what we know of Jesus is good. We have seen His power amongst us. Yes, yes," he went on mostly to himself, "even this teaching about beer-drinking is wise. What good does it bring us?"

There was silence in the room. The committee man rose. "Sit well," he said as he strolled toward the door leading to the long-house verandah. The people in the room all rose to leave.

Not wishing to appear as though they were hiding, Ding and his friend moved to the doorway between the two rooms. The village elder and his wife came into the room and nodded briefly to them. Ding waited for Lihan who remained in the middle of the room speaking to Usun. He could not see her, but he noticed a triumphant smirk on Anyi's face. Instinctively he knew that Lihan was urging Usun to come and that Usun was refusing. He clenched his fists.

Lihan spoke again. His voice was low and Ding strained

to catch what he said. Once again Ding marvelled at Lihan's composure. He knew that Lihan was taking a stand on his behalf. Was it courage or recklessness?

Ding shifted his gaze to Anyi again. He was enjoying himself. Usun had obviously refused to go with Lihan again. Lihan stood, uncertain as to what to do.

It was the witch-doctor who rescued him from his dilemma. "It is enough," he said to his son. "Go home child," he ordered Usun.

Without another word Lihan headed for the door and spoke to Ding, who in his concern for Usun, ignored him. Dejected, Lihan went on. Usun came out of the room, but looked straight through Ding and went on her way. He turned to follow her and saw the amused stares of Anyi's relatives. He flushed. Something was very amiss in his courtship and he didn't know how to manage it.

21

"HAVE you heard anything about Bungan?"

"Yes, I have heard," replied Ding non-committally. The family were sitting in their farm hut resting. They had been weeding their rice plot all the morning. Now the sun was a ball of fire above them.

"What do you know about it?" asked his father.

"Oh nothing much," said Ding and told his father what he had heard the night before.

His father frowned. "I don't like the sound of that," he remarked. "We Kayan are not men of two hearts. We have decided to follow Jesus. The witchdoctor is trying to make trouble."

"If only the missionary would come and teach us," sighed his mother.

It was a well worn refrain and Ding was tired of hearing it, tired of saying it and tired of thinking it.

"Yes, we do need the missionary to come," said Ding's father. "But don't let us waver. We have seen the power of Jesus. The spirits are obviously afraid of Him and we have no reason to doubt His care for us."

Ding admired his father. He didn't know very much about following Jesus, but what he knew he believed. He was an encouragement to Ding.

"I love Jesus," mumbled young Imang through a mouthful of sugar cane. "He saved me from the woman with the lumpy ears."

Ding looked affectionately at his little brother.

"Look at our rice," went on their father. "We can expect a good harvest." Ding looked out over the rice farm. There were plenty of weeds, but the family could cope with them. "We have had honey birds fly across our path, we have seen snakes and other bad omens of the past," went on his father, "but we have not been concerned. We know we have nothing to fear from these things. True there are monkeys who want to steal our grain and birds too, but we can cope with these. We are not afraid of them."

Ding picked up a bamboo container of water and drank thirstily. The others followed suit.

"Come on," said their father, "we have rested long enough." They went back to their weeding, except for Imang, who continued gnawing his lengthy piece of sugar cane.

Ding's thoughts returned to the night before. He had been rude to Lihan. His friend had tried to speak to him but he had pushed past. Thinking about it now Ding knew that it was partly because he wanted to catch up with Usun, but also because he resented Lihan's apparent friendliness with the witch-doctor.

Ding sighed as he weeded. He didn't feel happy. It wasn't only that he was troubled about Usun, but also he felt that rudeness did not please Jesus. He must go and see Lihan tonight.

"You have many thoughts, my son." Ding looked over at his mother weeding near him. Mujan and his father were further afield.

"Yes, many thoughts," agreed Ding. "Have you been talking, mother?"

"I have been talking," she answered, understanding his meaning.

"What is the news?"

"Is there news, I wonder." His mother paused. "There is something strange—hard to understand."

"Her parents are happy?" asked Ding.

"They are happy," replied his mother.

So, thought Ding, this is nothing to do with relatives. This comes from Usun herself.

"Why this strangeness, I wonder?" said Ding.

"It is a strangeness not understood," his mother informed him. "Her parents cannot understand her. They are concerned. They have spoken to her of her behaviour, but she is as one who is deaf."

"What of our marriage?" asked Ding, "I would like it to be soon."

"Her mother said to go slowly. This is not the time. Wait until this strangeness passes," advised his mother.

"Will it pass?" Anxiety edged Ding's voice. He had been sure of Usun. They had been promised to each other since childhood. In the past year, he had paid her more attention and she had responded, but now things had changed. She was distant and obviously interested in somebody else. "And it had to be Anyi, of all people," thought Ding bitterly.

What if Usun were to refuse him and marry Anyi? Ding squirmed at the thought of it. It was the humiliation of her not wanting him that hurt. "But she will have to marry me if our parents insist," he thought. A promise such as had been made by their parents was binding, whatever their personal feelings might be.

"On the other hand," he thought, "if she wants Anyi, life is going to be rather miserable." He thought of Lihan who had been forced to marry someone he didn't want. He couldn't imagine Usun being like Urei. No, Usun wouldn't nag. She wouldn't say anything. She would just look straight through him as if he wasn't there. What kind of life would that be?

Ding sighed. His mother hadn't answered his question which was a bad sign.

The sun was slipping behind the mountains as the family made their way back to the hut.

As they pulled into the bank at Long Nanga, Ding heard a shout. Looking around he saw some of his friends riding the rapids. "Come on!" they shouted.

Ding helped the family secure the canoe and went off to join his friends. Being carried down the rapids by the waves was exciting. It had its dangers as there could be nasty gashes from the rocks and occasionally there was a broken bone or two. But the Long Nangah rapids were not dangerous when the river was at its normal level. However, one needed to be a strong swimmer to get out of the current at the end.

Imang watched Ding go with longing eyes. "Not yet, child," said his father, seeing the look and knowing Imang's daring. "When you are older."

Imang sighed. Would he ever get older? Time moved so slowly.

Arriving at the end of the rapid Ding was turning to swim for the shore when he heard a voice beside him. "It's Taban Telepat . . . Ding."

Looking around, Ding saw a thin young lad swimming swiftly to shore. He recognised the boy as Ngau, a slave-class boy of Anyi's room. The government had banned slavery, but some people, while pretending to follow the government ruling, continued to have slaves.

"Taban Telepat . . ." Ding said it slowly to himself. What had the boy meant? He was obviously trying to help Ding in some way and was afraid that Anyi might find out. But what did he mean? Puzzling over the boy's words Ding swam slowly to the bank.

Ding was still musing over the words that evening as he started to go through to Lihan's room. On the way, he was passing through the room of widow Bulan La'ing. The old lady was sitting beside a tiny resin lamp threading beads. Ding paused and his eyes searched the darkness, but there didn't seem to be anyone else about. Impulsively, he went and sat near her.

Widow Bulan had been a witch-doctor. She had never wanted to be one and when a spirit had wanted to possess her she had refused. Her younger sister had then gone mad and her mother had been on the point of death. Other witch-doctors told her that this was the revenge of the spirit world and if she didn't accept the spirit who wanted to possess her, her mother would die and other calamities would fall upon the family. Reluctantly, she had consented and become a medium for the evil spirit.

Widow Bulan had received the news of Jesus with joy. She had declared that if no one else was going to follow, she was. When the whole house decided to follow, she was one who, like Ding's father, had asked questions of the missionary and could remember many of the answers.

In these past months Bulan had been loud in her praise of the Jesus way.

Watching her now as she tried to thread tiny beads by the feeble resin light, Ding wondered if he should ask her about Taban Telepat. She was well versed in Satan's medicine.

"Is it well with you my son?" she said softly.

Ding didn't answer her question. Instead he asked her, "Mother, what is Taban Telepat . . .?"

She looked up at him sharply. "Why do you ask?"

Ding was not prepared for her question. "I . . . I heard the name," he stammered.

"Hmm, yes it could be," the old lady said, half to herself. "A love potion," she said, giving Ding another piercing look before threading more beads. "Taban Telepat is a love potion," she explained.

"A love potion!" Ding exclaimed. "But . . ." His mind whirled. He had heard of such things vaguely. Was that what Ngau had been trying to tell him? Had Anyi been using a love potion on Usun? But where would he get it? How did it work?

"Yes, yes," muttered the old lady, "it could account for the strangeness."

Ding didn't ask her what she meant or how she knew. There were few secrets in a long-house and an old lady like Widow Bulan would know all that was going on.

"The boy was downriver with his father recently," she went on. "There is a very powerful witch-doctor at Long Kayo'. He is noted for his power at match-making."

"But what can I do?" Ding asked. "How does this medicine work?"

"It is in the form of a liquid," explained the ex-witch-doctor. "If Anyi bought some of this, and it has a very high price, he would see that it was sprinkled on something belonging to the girl, or put in something she drank, or even rubbed on her. He probably used the sprinkling method. That would be easier for him to do without her knowing."

"And it really works?" questioned Ding.

"Indeed it does." Bulan stopped threading beads for a moment. "Satan's medicine is very powerful, my son," she said. "It is well for us that the Lord Jesus really is more powerful than Satan—otherwise things would be very hard for us."

"What can I do if this love potion has been used on Usun, Mother?" asked Ding. Bulan stopped threading the beads and sat back thoughtfully. "I don't know," she said slowly. "If we were still in our old custom I could get in touch with the evil spirits but . . .," her voice trailed off.

Ding waited.

"Let me think about it child," she said finally. "I am sure Jesus has the answer. I will try and remember all the missionary said; perhaps there will be something that will help."

"You remember so many things that the missionary said." Ding was sincere in his praise.

"We witch-doctors are trained to remember," answered Widow Bulan. "If I could remember for the spirits, why not for Jesus?"

"I will come again," Ding said after a few minutes of silence. "Sit well, Mother."

"Go well, my son," answered the old lady. "Do not be concerned. Jesus is greater than Satan."

Ding went on through the rooms to Lihan. Widow Bulan had certainly given him something to think about.

22

As Ding arrived in his friend's room he found that he was about to leave on a wild pig hunt with his brother-in-law.

When Lihan saw Ding he looked a little uncertain. Ding walked over to him casually. He could see by the spear and wood flame-torch in Lihan's hand that he was going pig hunting and he felt a little hurt that he had not been invited. Then he remembered his behaviour of the night before.

Ding tugged at his hair. "Sorry I was so rude last night," he said. Lihan's face relaxed into a smile. "Come on. Let's catch some pigs," he grinned.

"I'll get my spear," Ding grinned back. "See you on the verandah." He did not speak to Urei who was sitting near the door of her tilung. She looked unhappy. Ding felt sorry for her.

Ding collected his spear and a piece of wood. The latter he smeared with resin to make a flame torch, then he joined Lihan and his brother-in-law. In spite of his problem with Usun, Ding felt almost light-hearted. It had been a long time since he had seen that boyish smile of Lihan's. His friend seemed to be his old self again.

The three men pushed off from the bank and paddled downriver for a short way. Then they tied the canoe to a tree and set off through the jungle.

Jau Wan, Lihan's brother-in-law, led the way. He was an older man, experienced in the ways of the jungle.

Suddenly he came to a halt in front and with a wave of his hand told those following him to do the same. They stopped and listened.

Ding could hear the excited snuffling of the dogs in the undergrowth to their left.

"The dogs are on to something," whispered Jau. "Spread out. You go to the right Lihan, you go to the left Ding, and I will take the middle." Before they could move there was a sudden roar, a thrashing and crashing in the bushes and a huge boar came charging by them. They didn't have time to raise a spear.

"Quick, after him." Jau was already dashing forward after the dogs which were hard on the boar's heels.

There was no path and the boar and dogs had the advantage of being able to race under the bushes.

"They've got him," shouted Jau as the barking of the dogs reached a crescendo. The three men hurried forward for the kill. The dogs apparently had the boar bailed up.

Suddenly the tone of the barking changed. "Aiyou! He is attacking the dogs! He must be a fierce one."

The agonised yelping continued and by the time the men reached the place where an injured dog lay, the boar had got away with three dogs still in hot pursuit.

Little sympathy was wasted on the hurt dog as they continued the chase. Frenzied barking told them that once again the dogs had the pig cornered.

Ding found himself close to the noise and shining his light before him found that the dogs had the pig bailed up against a large tree. The pig snorted and stamped. It was dazzled by the light and bewildered. Ding could hear the others crashing through the jungle behind him.

Keeping his resin lamp shining in the face of the ill-fated pig, Ding closed in. Suddenly Jau was beside him. "I'll keep him dazzled,—you get him," said Jau.

"That's decent of him," thought Ding.

He worked his way around to one side of the pig and suddenly lunged forward, thrusting his spear deep into its throat.

The boar made a half-hearted effort to fight then fell dead. It was a good kill.

"Well done, Ding," said Jau.

"That was a strong thrust," commented Lihan. He had tripped over a tree root and just arrived as Ding speared the beast. Had he been there Jau would have allowed him to kill it. But he was sincere in his praise of Ding.

"Let's cut it up and get home," said Jau. Together they quartered the animal and stuffed the pieces into their baskets. Slipping the baskets on their backs, they made for home. "You know, if we had been following the old custom we would never have got here tonight. We would have been too scared of all the omens," remarked Jau.

It surprised Ding to hear him speak in that way for he knew him to be a man who had little to say. Also he had imagined that he had followed the way of his in-laws in regard to the Jesus way.

"Yes," agreed Lihan. "We may not know much about Jesus, but what we know is good. It will be wonderful when we can know more. There are so many questions I would like to ask."

Again Ding was surprised. Lihan sounded like his normal happy self. No, not quite his old self, thought Ding. There is a change. He seems older, but he sounds happier. Ding wondered what had happened to lighten the heaviness he knew Lihan had felt after the baby's death.

"I don't know why this missionary is so long coming back," went on Jau. "This news of Jesus seems so wonderful and there is so much more for us to learn. You would think with that kind of news he would want to get back to us quickly."

Again Ding marvelled. It hadn't occurred to him that men like Jau would think like that.

They plodded on in silence until they reached their canoe.

As they stepped into it Jau spoke again. "What does your father say, Ding?" he asked. "Does he think the missionary will come back?"

"Yes he does," replied Ding. "The missionary said before he left that he was coming back. He also said he wanted us to have God's Book in our own language and that it would mean spending a lot of time with us to get it written down."

"Hmmmm, funny how all those little marks on that paper stuff speak," remarked Jau. "I wonder how God gave them that Book," he went on. "I wonder why he didn't give it to us too."

"Maybe He doesn't know our language," suggested Lihan. "He must know our language," said Ding, "or it would be no use praying."

"Of course," Lihan laughed at his own foolishness. "Anyway, the missionary said that God knows everything."

"Do you think that the missionary met God and He gave him the Book?" asked Jau.

"I don't think so," said Ding.

"Jesus died many, many harvests ago," said Lihan. "Did God give someone the Book right then?"

"Was there only one Book?" asked Jau.

"I don't know," said Ding. "Maybe He gave just the one Book and everyone else had to copy it."

"I shouldn't think there would be many?"

"There's ours and the Kenya, the Kelabit, the Lun Bawang, the Iban, the Penan, the Chinese, the Malay, and the European. That's nine."

"There is Japanese too," remarked Jau, who had been down-river once during the war when the Japanese invaded Borneo.

"Yes, I had forgotten," said Ding. He had seen the Japanese. Ding wanted to ask him about it, but Lihan continued their conversation.

"Do you think the Book the missionary had is the only one?"

"From what he said it is the only Book God has given. I know there are other books. I have seen them down-river. The Chinese have them," said Jau.

"Do they read too?" asked Lihan.

"Yes, indeed they do. They are clever, the Chinese," Jau informed him.

They were pulling into the bank and the conversation ended. Lihan and his brother-in-law went to their room and Ding went to his.

As he lay down on his mat to sleep he felt relaxed. His mother was cooking the pig and the delicious aroma made his mouth water. It had been a pleasant and profitable evening. He would have liked to talk to Lihan about Usun and what Bulan had said. Never mind, it could wait. He was glad to have got to know Jau a little. Also it was good to see Lihan looking so much happier. He must ask him what had happened.

For the moment the powers of satanic charms and the threat of the Bungan cult were minor details—but not for long.

23

I⊤ is good to go off to work with a satisfying meal of wild pig and rice inside you, thought Ding. He and his family were paddling up-river to their farm for the day's weeding. As they arrived at the top of the first rapid, Ding saw that Usun with her family were just pulling out from the shore a few strokes upstream. They had been collecting some horse-mangoes which had fallen from their tree overnight.

Usun's father hailed them and pulled over beside them to share the horse-mangoes.

"Quite a few fell last night," he remarked jovially. "Just as well we got here before the others."

Ding knew he was referring to Anyi's family. They were clever at finding other people's fruit on the ground. They weren't past giving a few branches a shake either, Ding thought.

The two canoes kept pace as they continued up the river. The two men talked about their farms and the weeding. Ding, who was in the front of their canoe, kept looking around trying to catch Usun's eye, but she pretended not to notice. Her young brother sniggered. Ding was so angry with both of them that he didn't see a big log come floating down. They were almost on top of it before he saw it and in trying to push it away Ding fell in.

For Imang the day was made. Ding dragged himself back into the canoe without a word. He resumed his place in the front of the canoe, back ramrod-straight, eyes straight ahead. Nothing was said. The men continued their conversation.

Ding was glad when, at the next rapid, Usun's family went up first and kept on going. He felt the humiliation of the whole incident. Not only that, but the whole problem of Usun and her rejection of him was opened up to him afresh. He spent the rest of the day brooding over Usun and being annoyed with Imang. The lively little boy delighted in giving frequent imitations of Ding falling overboard.

That evening Lihan came to Ding's room before the family had finished their meal.

"Come and eat," said Ding's mother.

"I have eaten," replied Lihan.

"Come and have some more," Ding invited him.

"I'm full," replied Lihan. "You eat slowly. Eat until you are full."

"Sit down," said Ding. "I'll be finished soon." Lihan hesitated and sat down.

After he had finished Ding came and sat beside his friend.

"How is your farm?" asked Ding.

"Plenty of weeds," said Lihan, "but otherwise doing well." Imang came rolling out of the tilung. Seeing Ding and Lihan sitting in the shadows he started to giggle and go through the antics of Ding falling out of the canoe.

Ding felt himself flushing. It had been bad enough all day. The incident was too painful to relate to his friend, but now Lihan looked at him with inquiring eyes.

"Go away, Imang," ordered Ding.

"Come here, Imang," called his mother from the tilung.

Imang was enjoying himself too much to be obedient until a sterner voice ordered him into the tilung. He obeyed. His father was not to be trifled with.

"What happened?" asked Lihan.

"It was nothing," replied Ding. "Have you noticed my friend's behaviour lately?" he went on, tugging at his hair.

"I have noticed," replied Lihan. "Why is it? Why should she be interested in Anyi? She knows she is engaged to you. She has always been a good girl. But now it is strange. Do you know why?"

"Not really," replied Ding and then went on to tell of his conversation with Widow Bulan.

"Aiyah!" exclaimed Lihan. "I never thought of that. I do remember hearing about the witch-doctor, but he is a long way downriver. I have not heard of anyone going to him. If it is true that Anyi has used this love potion on Usun what can you do about it?"

"I don't know. But Widow Bulan said I should wait till she herself can think it through. She knew what to do when she was a witch-doctor, but she doesn't know what to do now that we are following Jesus."

"Being a follower of Jesus certainly hasn't changed Anyi's family," remarked Lihan.

"No, but then they do not really follow," replied Ding.

"It is as the missionary said, 'When the harvest is nearly ripe we find that many of the husks are empty.' Yes, it is a good parable."

"I was surprised to see you in the witch-doctor's room the other night," Ding said, trying to sound casual.

Lihan was silent for a minute and then he spoke. "You know, something happened the other night. It's hard to explain," he said cracking his knuckle joints thoughtfully.

"The baby . . . all that business. It was terrible. I felt as though I wanted to die. I was angry with the missionary for not being there. I was angry with the Lord Jesus too for not helping us in some way. I wanted to talk to you but I couldn't. Listening to that baby die. Aiyah!" He put his hands over his face. "Ding it was awful. I didn't feel it was right but each time I spoke everyone silenced me. 'Such a child was destined to grow up and kill someone,' they said. 'It might be you or your wife or your other children. What about that?'" Lihan paused and sighed, "I didn't have any real argument. I just agreed with your father that it didn't seem to be the Jesus Way."

A man came looking for Ding's father. Ding called his

father who came out of the tilung and went out of the room. Lihan continued, "Anyi's father came in a few times. He was always hinting about not having anyone to teach us. A couple of times he spoke about Bungan. I pretended not to be interested but my father-in-law asked a few questions. I began to wonder if perhaps it wouldn't be better to follow this 'Bungan.' Anyi's father seems to know what to do. Also, there was someone downriver willing to come up and teach us. There didn't seem to be much to it."

"Is your father-in-law really interested?" Ding cut in with the question.

"I am not sure," replied Lihan. "Anyway he had been out hunting and caught a pig," he went on. "He wanted to send some down to the witch-doctor's room. I said I would take it. When I got to his room, there were a few folk there including Usun. So I thought I would see what I could find out. I just felt so miserable about everything."

Ding remembered that Lihan's father-in-law had said he didn't know where Lihan was that night. He obviously hadn't wanted Ding to know.

"And what happened?" Ding was anxious to hear the end of the story.

"Well, when Anyi's father was talking about sacrificing fowls and eggs, you know what came into my mind?"

"No," said Ding.

"I thought of that verse the missionary taught us: 'For God loved the world so much that He gave His only Son so that anyone who believes in Him shall not perish but have eternal life.'"

He said it slowly and carefully and it seemed to Ding, with a touch of awe.

"And then," Lihan seemed at a loss for words, "then . . . I can't explain it, but all this about sacrificing eggs and fowls seemed wrong and useless."

Again he paused as if searching for words. "I just knew somehow that Jesus cared for me and although I didn't understand about the baby and all that, I could trust Him."

"I knew there was something different about you," exclaimed Ding. "I didn't know what had happened."

"What were you doing there anyway?" Lihan asked.

"I was looking for you and Usun," answered Ding.

"You don't think Anyi would ask for Usun, do you?" asked Lihan, returning to the subject of Usun.

"It would be very bad custom if he did," replied Ding. "But then Anyi was never one for worrying about custom."

"You know," said Lihan. "Anyi and his family have always been able to get what they wanted because we have been afraid of his father's power. Now we have a power greater than that. They can't get all their own way."

"That's true," agreed Ding. "But you know, if Usun doesn't want to marry me what is the use of getting married? I know her parents could make her marry me but we wouldn't have any regard for each other, and we would be miserable." He was going to add "like you and Urei," but thought better of it.

"Yes it's awful being forced to marry someone you don't want to," agreed Lihan. "That's another thing Ding. You know how I hated Urei. Well that's all gone. She didn't want to follow the old custom about the baby either. Then she became so ill from sitting close to the fire. Somehow with all the trouble, she stopped nagging and we got to talking. She was saying she wanted to know more about what the missionary meant when he said Jesus died for our sins. We have had some good talks together."

Ding was silent for a moment. "You know Lihan, even though we do know so little about Jesus, what we know does make a difference, doesn't it." It was more of a statement than a question. "It certainly makes you want to know more."

24

"Siho', Siho'."

The words burned into Ding's brain as he automatically staggered to his feet from a sound sleep. He was already at the door of their room, nearly falling over his father in a headlong rush before the significance of the word struck him.

He followed his father out the door and joined the excited, yelling crowd of men streaming past. In spite of the noise of the pounding feet and agitated voices Ding could hear another noise—the roar of flood waters. A cloud-burst upstream was bringing a flash flood. Canoes must be secured swiftly or they would be swept away. Ding's feet hardly touched the notched pole as he ran for the river. The "Siho'", a tremendous wall of powerful water, was nearly upon them.

Ding was thankful for a full moon. He didn't have time to appreciate its beauty but it helped them all to see what they were doing.

Ding and his father picked up their canoe and made for the long-house. It was heavy and they staggered under their load. Two men appeared from somewhere to help them.

After dumping it on the long-house verandah they all ran for the river again. There were other canoes not yet carried up.

Squealing pigs and squawking fowls now added to the general din as they were unceremoniously tossed onto the long verandah. Children screamed in fear, not knowing what was happening but aware of impending calamity. As Ding and his father, with another man, lifted yet another canoe and prepared to make for the long-house they saw the great wall of water come rushing around the bend. They dropped the canoe and ran for their lives. At that point, Ding tripped.

Ding's father had reached the safety of the verandah before he realised that Ding was not behind him. "Where's Ding?" he exclaimed and turned back. Two men grabbed him and others came to help as they realised his intention. He struggled and pleaded with them to let him go. But they knew he had no hope of helping Ding and held him fast.

"The house is going to collapse," someone cried. It was creaking and groaning as the water swirled underneath, rising higher and higher.

"Take to the canoes," someone yelled.

"No," cried another, "we would all be drowned."

"We'll be drowned anyway."

"Take to the canoes while there's time."

"There's still hope. It may not rise further."

"It is still rising."

"To the canoes!"

"No! Wait!"

Some were preparing to put canoes over the side. No one knew who started it, but suddenly the cry was taken up—"Pray! Pray to the Lord Jesus." There were many there that night who had often said they didn't know how to pray and always left it to the few, but they soon found their voices. Panic was dissolved as they began calling on the Lord to help them.

"Look!" someone said. "The water is going down." A stillness swept over the people and even the pigs and fowls grew quiet. Everyone watched in awe. The water was going down, very slowly to be sure, but the danger was past.

Ding's father had become quiet too. In his anguish he had prayed to the Lord Jesus, "Save my son, save my son." He looked at the water, still swirling powerfully over the undergrowth and wondered how the Lord Jesus could possibly answer his prayer.

The men slowly loosed their grip on Ding's father. Together they prepared to launch a canoe. A whisper swept through the crowd. "Ding Juk drowned in the Siho'." Lihan heard it and felt sick. Ding must be dead. He couldn't have survived a siho' as big as that.

Ding was not dead. He was not hurt when he fell and it was only a brief delay. However he knew he could not reach the long-house in time. With the agility of a frightened monkey he shinned up the nearest coconut tree. He was half way up when the wall of water hit the tree. A huge wave of water splashed over him. The tree bent over with the force of the water and Ding had to hold on for dear life. Just below him the water swirled and sucked and gurgled around the jungle undergrowth. He caught a glimpse of the long-house and could see the water rising under it.

The main wall of water had passed but the whole area was flooded. From his precarious position Ding could see the swollen river reaching into the jungle. It was still rising and was frightening to see.

Ding's arms and legs were aching as he clung tenaciously to the swaying tree. From the long-house came a melee of sounds. He knew the people were worried about the rising waters. Then he heard the tone of their voices change and they became quiet.

Ding caught an occasional glimpse of the long-house through the trees. He gathered that some canoes were being launched. He wondered why, not thinking that they would be searching for him.

In the long-house the people stood silently waiting. Among them stood Usun, white-faced and bewildered. She had heard the whispered "Ding Juk has been drowned," and she felt a great sorrow. There was something else too. She shook her head as if trying to shake something away, but there was a darkness and confusion in her mind that she didn't understand.

Ding saw a canoe emerge below him. He tried to call out but his throat seemed numb and no sound came. He felt he couldn't hold on much longer. "Help me, Lord Jesus," he whispered. "Help me."

The canoe had passed by, another emerged, and as it did so one of the men looked up. "He's there," he yelled at the top of his voice, pointing to the tree.

One of the men caught hold of the tree as the others held the canoe against the strong current with their paddles. "Slide down, Ding," they called.

Ding was so numb he felt he would fall if he let go. Suddenly he was aware that one of the men had climbed up behind him. Slowly he began to work his numb fingers and feet and to slide down the tree. The man behind gave him some support. Reaching the canoe he was helped in by willing hands.

Along the long-house the cry had been taken up. "Ding is found. He is alive."

The other canoes came alongside the canoe where Ding sat. Everyone was asking questions but for the moment Ding was too exhausted to answer. In one of the canoes he saw his father and as their eyes met Ding saw that his father's face was wet with tears. Only then did Ding realise that people had thought he was drowned.

People were returning to their rooms now. Some of the men remained on the verandah to tie up pigs and make sure there was no further danger.

As Ding laid his aching body on the mat there came a loud yawn. Imang sat up. He had slept in his mother's arms through all the noise and tumult. "I'm hungry," he said.

"The dawn is a long way off," his mother said. "Go back to sleep."

Imang looked sleepily at his parents and Mujan sitting by the fire. Outside he could hear the grunts and squeals of pigs. "It is morning," he pouted. "I'm hungry."

"It is time to sleep," his father said sternly.

Ding didn't hear the end of the argument. He drifted off to sleep, comforted by the concern he had seen in Usun's eyes as he was helped onto the verandah.

25

Ding woke late the next morning. Apart from stiffness in some of his muscles he felt no ill effects from his adventure. The room was empty. Stretching himself he wandered onto the verandah. People were everywhere discussing the siho'. Everyone except old Jelivang agreed that it was the worst in their experience. He remembered a siho' in which the long-house had actually collapsed. Many people had been drowned. Some had managed to cling to canoes or trees and had been saved. He was a good story teller and had an attentive audience most of the morning.

Folk came crowding around Ding. "Tell us what happened," they asked.

"Did you really ride on a crocodile's back, Ding?" asked Imang wide-eyed. Everyone laughed, but some looked at Ding as though they thought there might be some truth in it.

"They say the siho' threw you up a tree?" said one of Ding's friends questioningly.

"Did you really get taken across the other side and then swim back?" asked another.

Ding smiled and proceeded to tell them what had really happened. It didn't make much difference. So many tales had already circulated that the truth was too tame. Ding was a hero.

The water had receded from under the long-house now and the pigs had plenty of mud in which to wallow. The verandah had been cleared of canoes which were now safely tethered to trees. The fowls were pecking their way through the debris. The river was still high and no one was venturing out. It was one thing to go out in an emergency, but skilled boatmen though they were, the Kayan were not foolhardy. Some people were bemoaning the loss of pigs, many of which had run for their lives when confronted by wildly excited people wanting to carry them onto the verandah. The fowls had been more fortunate. They were usually put into bamboo baskets each night and strung up under the long-house. It had been easier to rescue them.

As Ding strolled down the long-house verandah with his friends one phrase kept recurring as everyone discussed the events of the night. "If the Lord Jesus had not answered our prayers we would have drowned."

Lihan came up, concern in his eyes. "Ding, I really thought you were dead last night. It was a terrible feeling. What happened?" Again Ding told his story as he would do several times more during the day. "The Lord Jesus certainly helped you, Ding," said Lihan. "He saved us all," he added soberly.

Ding's purpose in strolling along was to find Usun. Had the events of last night changed her? Was Anyi really using a love potion and did it really have the power to make her want him? Again Ding thought of the concern in Usun's eyes as he had been carried onto the verandah.

Someone else had noticed Usun's anxiety. Anyi had not been pleased. As he moved dejectedly from the crowd he knew that something must be done. He hoped his witch-doctor father would have an answer. Perhaps some more taban telepat was needed.

Ding saw Usun winnowing rice with her mother. Feigning interest in the river he went to the verandah rails and looked out. Then he turned back and spoke to his friends and as he did so his eyes met Usun's. It was only a glance, but in that moment he knew that her interest in him had been renewed. He turned back to the rails and commented again on the flooded river to his friends. Inwardly he felt a quiet happiness. He must visit her family tonight.

Sitting on the rail further down the verandah, Anyi

smiled maliciously to himself. He had noted the interchange of looks. "We'll see, my friend, we'll see!" he muttered spitefully.

When he had finished his evening meal Ding took his guitar and wandered through the rooms. He paused at Widow Bulan's room and sat down near her as she worked on her beads. She waited for him to speak. "It is well, mother," he said softly. He could hear her son moving about in the tilung.

Widow Bulan shot him a quizzical glance. "It is well?" she questioned.

"It is well, mother," Ding repeated. "Do not be concerned."

Again the quizzical look. "Are you sure?"

"I am sure," said Ding confidently.

"Be careful, my son. These things are not quickly settled."

"I will take care," replied Ding, but a faint uneasiness stirred in him. Widow Bulan was a wise woman. He knew that in spite of her calm words she was giving him a strong warning.

"Sit well, mother," he said after a few minutes.

"Go well, my son," she replied.

Arriving in Usun's room Ding was disappointed to find it empty except for Usun's mother. She looked up as he entered and then looked down again quickly at the mat she was making. Ding's uneasiness grew. "Where is Usun?" he asked politely.

"Where is she, I wonder?" Ding was sure she knew. He sat down near her.

"All is not well?" questioned Ding after a few minutes of silence. Usun's mother sighed. "All is not well."

"I thought things were well this morning."

"They were well this morning."

"They are not well now?"

"No, they are not well now."

"Why?"

"Why I wonder. Who knows why?"

Ding was baffled. He was sure Usun's mother was telling the truth. She had obviously noticed the change in her daughter this morning, but now it seemed that something had happened to change her again. Even her mother didn't know why.

Just then Usun came into the room with two of her friends. They were giggling in a way that irritated Ding.

When Usun saw Ding she paused. The giggling stopped. Without another look at him she glided gracefully onto the mat in the corner of her room. Her friends followed. They resumed their giggling, ignoring Ding completely.

Ding rose abruptly and left the room. He was fuming. Instead of going through the rooms he went onto the verandah. Some of his friends were there. He joined them as they strolled down the long-house verandah. He didn't speak, and they, sensing something was wrong, were silent. One of them strummed softly on his guitar. Ding carried his own guitar but he did not have the heart to play.

As they passed Widow Bulan's door, Ding paused. Then without a word of explanation he opened the door and went in, closing it behind him. His friends looked at one another, shrugged and strolled on.

Widow Bulan was still sitting with her beads when Ding entered. She looked up at him as he came in at the door. "Sit down," was all she said and went on with her work.

Ding sat for a few minutes in silence. "It is not well," he said at last.

"It is not well," she repeated as if she had expected that.

"What can I do, mother?" asked Ding desperately.

"I have been thinking," said Bulan after a while. "The missionary told us to pray about everything. He told us that the Lord Jesus would always hear us." She paused. "No. He said that we must first ask Jesus to forgive our sins. We mustn't have bad things in our hearts.

Then the Lord Jesus would help us." Again she paused and looked at Ding. "Have you a clean heart my son?" she asked.

"I am angry," said Ding after a slight pause.

"You must ask the Lord Jesus to take away your anger. We know that Jesus is greater than Satan," the old lady continued, "so if we ask Him to help us He will. He can take away your anger and break the power of the love potion that is affecting Usun."

"You mean just by our praying the taban telepat won't have any more power?" asked Ding doubtfully. He knew the Lord Jesus could take away his anger, but he wondered about Him breaking the power of the love potion. Of course He was greater than Satan. But was a simple prayer enough?

"Yes," agreed Widow Bulan. "We have seen Jesus answer prayer about many things. Think how He answered our prayers last night. Yes, He answers prayer. I am sure He will answer prayer about the love potion. It is a wrong thing and He is One who knows what to do about wrong things."

"You are right, Mother," agreed Ding. "But it sounds so simple."

Widow Bulan sniffed. "Of course it's simple. The Lord Jesus is very great. I don't know just how great but He certainly has great power."

There was something else troubling Ding.

"Mother, do you remember the missionary teaching that God has a wife?" Ding had been wanting to ask the question ever since he had heard the conversation in Anyi's room.

"A wife!" exclaimed Bulan. "No I don't think I heard him mention a wife. No," she said adamantly, "he didn't mention a wife. I am sure I would have remembered." She paused, frowning. "He did try to explain something to us. Jesus is God." She paused and put down the bead-

work. "But He is also the Son of God." She was silent
again. "I don't understand it," she said finally. "But God
didn't have a wife." She shot Ding a questioning glance.
"What have you been hearing?"

Ding knew that she would have heard of Bungan. "I
have heard of some one called 'Bungan, the wife of God',"
he answered.

Widow Bulan snorted. "Huh! There are those who
seek their own ends. They will believe anything," she said.
"If God had a wife the missionary would have told us.
No. This matter of Jesus being God is bigger than we know.
I would like to know more," she ended wistfully.

"When the missionary comes there will be no end to our
questions," said Ding.

"He must come soon," Widow Bulan replied. "What we
know is good, but we need to know more. We do not want
to know more of 'Bungan.' We want to know more of
Jesus. We must have The Book too. The missionary said
that The Book was more important than he himself."

They sat for a while in silence. Then Ding spoke: "So
you think I should ask the Lord Jesus to break this power?"
he questioned.

"Yes, that is right, my son. You ask Him tonight; tomorrow all will be well."

It sounded too easy to Ding. On the other hand when he
remembered the way Jesus had answered their prayer for
Imang and regarding the flood, and other matters, he
felt hopeful. Nothing was too hard for the Lord Jesus.

"Sit well, mother," said Ding as he rose to go.

"Go well, my son," she answered. "I too will pray."

26

THE hour was late—too late for Ding to visit Usun. He sighed. He would have to wait till tomorrow. Before he slept Ding prayed and asked the Lord Jesus to break the power of the love potion on Usun. The next day was Sunday and Ding and his family gathered with the rest of the people for a meeting on the long-house verandah. Usually this meeting wasn't much different to the early morning meetings. The missionary had told them that on this day Christians all over the world met to worship God. They sang and read God's Word and someone taught them. One day they would be able to worship in the same way, the missionary had said.

Ding craned his neck to see Usun. He saw her near the front—her back towards him. Ding's father led the meeting that morning and told them how thankful he was that God had answered his prayer for Ding. He also reminded them how the Lord Jesus had answered all their prayers when the flood came.

He went on to say that it was true they didn't know very much about Jesus and they didn't have the Book, but what they did know was reassuring. He exhorted them not to waver but to remember that their lives were much happier than they had been. He finished up with another reminder of the things the Lord Jesus had done for them.

After the meeting Ding went off to see Lihan. Usun had gone to the river with a bevy of girls.

Sunday was difficult in some ways. The missionary had taught them not to work. It was a day of rest. But everyone found doing nothing very hard. When there were so many baskets to be mended, ropes to be spliced, wood to be chopped and many other things crying out to be done, sitting around wasn't easy.

The missionary had said that it was a day for studying the Book, but they didn't have the Book. In any case only a very few could read.

Lihan was sitting talking to Urei when Ding walked in. She looked up at Ding and smiled faintly. Ding couldn't remember Urei really smiling before. "She looks quite nice," he thought. He sat down a little way away from them.

"Have you heard that Anyi's father is going down river again?" asked Lihan.

"No, I hadn't heard," replied Ding. "Why is he going?" Trips downriver were rare and it was unusual for anyone to go twice in a year.

"Why is he going, I wonder," mused Lihan. "Some say to trade. But to trade what?"

"He can't be taking rice," said Ding. "He wouldn't have enough to eat. He hasn't had any time to make jungle rope or gather resin from the forest. He took those things last time."

"Perhaps it has something to do with 'Bungan'," remarked Lihan.

"Perhaps," said Ding. "Perhaps he is going to learn more about his new Bungan cult. Still, it will be an expensive trip if he has nothing to trade," he added.

"The ways of the witch-doctor are past knowing," remarked Urei. "He will try and turn us from the Lord Jesus."

Ding was surprised to hear her speak. She had never joined in a conversation between Lihan and him before. Unless you counted the occasional sarcastic remark aimed at Lihan as conversation.

"Yes, that is his aim," agreed Ding.

"I wondered if he was going to bring one of those Bungan witch-doctors up here," remarked Lihan.

"What! And try to persuade the whole long-house to turn to Bungan?" Ding looked at Lihan open-mouthed.

"He might try to do that, you know," said Lihan.

"But most people in the long-house are happy that we are following Jesus."

"Yes, but they are also restless and disappointed that the missionary hasn't come."

"I think your father is right, Ding," said Urei. "We shouldn't waver just because the missionary hasn't come. The Lord Jesus has answered our prayers in many ways. We don't have to live in fear of Him. We know He loves us."

Again Ding was amazed at the change in Urei. Surely this must be something the Lord Jesus had done. She seemed so different, now.

"I hope everyone will realise that," said Lihan. "It would be a dreadful thing if we changed to the 'Bungan' custom."

"I wouldn't change," said Ding adamantly. "Only those who were not sincere in the beginning would turn back."

"We must pray more earnestly that the missionary will come," said Lihan. "When we have the Book in our own language we will have the answers to Bungan and the like." Lihan's mention of prayer brought Ding's thoughts back to Usun. She should be back from the river. Abruptly he rose. "Sit well," he said.

"Go well," replied Lihan and Urei together. They were a little mystified by his hasty departure.

Ding wandered onto the verandah. He looked up and down. Usun was not there. He walked down the verandah and rather self-consciously opened the door of Usun's room and went in. Usun was alone in the room but he could hear movement in the tilung.

Usun looked up when Ding came in but looked down

again quickly. Hopefully Ding sat down a little way away from her, although he hadn't been invited. There was silence. Movement had ceased in the tilung. No doubt Usun's mother was listening intently.

Ding cleared his throat. He had never been alone with Usun before and he felt somewhat abashed. "The river has gone down," he said lamely, wanting to strike up a conversation. No answer. Ding felt himself flushing. He tried again. "Did you lose any pigs in the flood?" No answer.

Was she just shy, as he was? That must be it. They weren't used to being alone. This had nothing to do with the love potion. Surely its power had been broken when he prayed to the Lord Jesus. But Ding only half convinced himself. If only she would look up or say something.

Perhaps a direct question would help. "Is it well with us?" Ding held his breath again for no answer was forthcoming. Silence. Usun's mother couldn't stand it any longer. "Answer him you foolish child," she called from within the tilung.

Usun obeyed and Ding was left in no doubt as to whether his prayer had been answered. "Go away," she said bluntly. "I don't want you."

When Ding reached his own room it was empty. He was glad as he wanted to be alone. He went into the tilung and closed the door.

Sitting on the mat in the darkness he tried to sort out his confused thoughts. He had been humiliated by Usun's rejection, especially so because he knew it would be known all over the long-house soon. Usun's mother would tell her friend, and that friend would tell her friend and gradually it would spread. There were few secrets in a long-house.

What concerned Ding more was that his prayer had not been answered. Was there a power greater than the

Lord Jesus? He remembered that Widow Bulan had said that the witch-doctor who prepared the love potion was very powerful. Was he more powerful than the Lord Jesus?

What else had Widow Bulan said? Ah yes, one must pray with a clean heart. He had asked the Lord Jesus to take away his anger and that prayer had been answered because he didn't feel angry any more. He couldn't think of anything else wrong in his heart. But this other prayer? Why had it not been answered?

That evening after the usual Sunday night meeting, Ding went to Widow Bulan's room. Her son, daughter-in-law and children were all there. They looked at Ding curiously. "Sit down," said Widow Bulan's son.

Ding sat in a corner as far from the family as possible. Widow Bulan came out of the tilung and sat near him.

There was silence. Widow Bulan was waiting for Ding to speak. So were her son and his wife, but Ding didn't want them to hear the conversation. Fortunately the children started quarrelling and made the baby cry. With this noise in the background Ding spoke. "Mother, my prayer was not answered. This witch-doctor downriver must be very powerful."

Widow Bulan frowned. "He is very powerful, but I am sure there are no witch-doctors as powerful as the Lord Jesus." She paused. "I wonder why your prayer was not answered."

"If only Anyi's father would love Jesus we would not have all this trouble," said Ding after a long silence. "He didn't want us to become Christians and he has been making trouble ever since."

Widow Bulan sighed. "Yes. It is a pity. He was a good man when he was young, but the love of power and possessions made him a willing tool for evil spirits."

For a moment Ding forgot his own problem. The idea of

the witch-doctor once being a good man was unbelievable. "A good man," he repeated incredulously.

"He was, he was indeed," affirmed Widow Bulan. There was a wistfulness about her that puzzled Ding. She sounded as though she had been fond of him. He would have liked to ask her more, but thought better of it.

Widow Bulan sighed again. "This problem you have. It is not Anyi's father. It is that the Lord Jesus has not answered our prayer. I can't understand it. I don't know what to do. I must think about it some more."

After the evening meal Ding stayed on in the tilung with his parents. Mujan went off to join some of her friends, particularly one of them who was a sister of Ngau Wan. Imang was lying on the floor fast asleep, his half eaten bundle of rice in his hand.

Ding did not enter into his parents' conversation. He wanted to tell his parents all that had happened about Usun, but he did not quite know how to broach the subject.

At last his father turned to him and said, "You are quiet my child. What is troubling you?"

Ding took the opportunity to tell his parents all that had happened, including his conversation with Widow Bulan. His father rubbed his chin thoughtfully. "I have heard this talk of love-potion being given to Usun. It would seem by her behaviour that there is some truth in it."

"Yes," agreed Ding's mother, "Usun is a good girl. But her mother said she has changed lately and they don't know what to make of it."

"I wonder why the Lord Jesus didn't break the spell when you asked him to," mused Ding's father.

Nobody knew the answer to that. Ding felt depressed.

27

DING and his family were returning from the farm rather early that afternoon. Mujan wasn't feeling well and Imang had cut himself on some bamboo. As the weeding was going well Ding's mother suggested that they go home. She also mentioned that there was very little wood left.

On their way downstream they met Lihan and his brother-in-law coming up-stream. "Where are you going?" Ding called.

"Going to get wood," Lihan called back.

"I'll come too," Ding told them. Immediately Lihan and Jau swung over towards the other canoe. Ding changed canoes and with an exchange of "go well" with his family, continued up-river with his friends.

They did not go far before securing their canoe to a tree and setting off into the jungle. After a short walk a suitable tree was found and they began to cut it down. It was hot work.

They busied themselves with chopping for a while. Then they tied the wood into bundles with jungle twine.

"I wonder if the Kelabit will bring any news of the missionary," Ding remarked as they stacked their wood into the canoe.

"They may have some news," said Lihan. "The last time they came they said the missionary was expected up there at full moon."

"That was a long time ago and we didn't hear if he came," said Ding.

They could see the two big canoes beached as they came into the river bank at Long Nanga. The Kelabit had arrived. So had a group of tribesmen. They were standing huddled together near the shore. Some of the Kayan were calling them in to bathe. It was a great joke for they all knew the Penan disliked the water and were poor swimmers.

One of the older men finished his bath and went and spoke kindly to the Penan. They followed him up to the long-house.

Later a number of folk gathered to chat to the Kelabit tribesmen. Visitors were rare at Long Nanga and when they came everyone liked to gather to hear news and exchange views. Being young, Ding and Lihan would not enter into the conversation, but they liked to hear what was said.

When they arrived the Kelabit were talking about rice. They always had a good crop for which they praised their good soil. There were about eight of them sitting there and after a while six more of their number joined them—big, strong-looking men, muscular and well built.

From rice the conversation turned to canoes and the dangers of the rapids. The Kelabit were not as skilled as the Kayan in river travel as they rarely travelled by river. However, what they lacked in skill, they made up in daring. As they related some of their experiences on the way downriver, the Kayan marvelled at their presumption while admiring their daring.

Ding enjoyed listening to the stories, but wished that someone would ask about the missionary.

While they were talking an elder strolled in. He looked at the Kelabit and then at his fellow Kayan. "Are they dogs?" he said indicating the visitors, "that we give them nothing to drink and no tobacco?" There was silence.

One of the Kelabit spoke up, a cheerful pleasant-faced man whom Ding knew as Raja Lejau, which meant King Tiger.

"At least that was his name the last time he was here," thought Ding. The Kelabit had a habit of changing their names on certain occasions mainly connected with the birth of their children and grandchildren.

"We Kelabit no longer drink that which makes the mind reel and the tongue foolish and bitter," he said pleasantly, "nor do we use that which makes the throat itch and racks the chest with coughing. Since we became Christians we have left these things."

"Huh!" exclaimed the elder as he sat down. "True it is not good to get drunk, but what is the harm in having a little rice beer to quench one's thirst and to give to one's visitors?"

"What harm indeed?" cried a mocking voice from the back. The elder had the grace to look uncomfortable. He could not stop at *a little*.

"And who is clever at drinking a little?" asked Raja Lejau looking questioningly around the room.

No one answered his question. Some looked sheepish.

One thought it prudent to change the subject. "What news of the one who teaches of the Lord Jesus?" he asked. Ding craned his neck, but could not see who it was. He didn't recognise the voice.

"Yes," said another, "we have been waiting for him to come. When is he coming?"

Raja Lejau looked surprised. "Haven't you heard that he had to return to his own country?"

"Gone home?" The exclamation came from Ding's father.

"Yes," said the Kelabit, "he is ill."

"He was in a prison camp when the Japanese were here," added another Kelabit whom Ding did not recognise. "He was badly treated and therefore never very strong after that. When he became ill it was necessary for him to go home."

"How long ago?"

"About five moons ago."

"He did not let us know."

"Are there no other missionaries?" Ding could tell his father was worried.

Raja Lejau wrinkled his nose. "Yes there are, but they are teaching in other places. The missionary sent us word to pray that more people would come from his country."

A murmur of voices arose around Ding. "How are we going to learn more about the Lord Jesus?"

"He said that he would come back."

"What about The Book he said we would have in our own language?"

"If we followed 'Bungan' at least we would know what to do."

"He should have sent word he wasn't coming back."

"Who would teach us about Bungan cult?"

"Akem Baya' knows someone who would come straight away."

Ding rose. He felt sick at heart. As he turned to go he saw Anyi watching him, smiling.

28

THE next morning as Ding and his family were getting into their canoe they saw that the Kelabit had already gone. They were noted for early departures. It was jokingly said that they stayed awake all night to make sure they got away before morning light.

Ding had slept restlessly. He awoke unhappy and depressed. There seemed to be no answer to the problem of Usun. The missionary wasn't coming. There was no one to teach them. Everyone was disappointed. The witch-doctor was planning to go and get someone to tell them about Bungan. The picture looked dismal.

As they paddled up-river these problems were churning themselves around in Ding's mind.

"Those Kelabit know some good stories from God's Book," remarked Ding's father, breaking into his son's troubled thoughts.

"Do they?" asked Ding in surprise.

"Yes. You should have stayed last night," remarked his father. "Raja Lejau told us several stories of how the Lord Jesus had helped sick people."

"I liked the story of the son who was lost," put in Ding's mother.

"What son?" asked Ding.

"I don't know what his name was, but he became very bad and ran away from home. Then when he was sorry for his wrong-doing he came home and found his father waiting for him and ready to forgive him. Raja Lejau said that it was a parable that the Lord Jesus told to help us understand God's great love for us."

As his parents went on talking about what the Kelabit had said, Ding was sorry he hadn't stayed. He and Mujan plied their parents with questions as they paddled.

Ding quite forgot about the missionary not coming until midday when they were sitting in their farm hut.

"All that the Kelabit people have told us is good," he said.

"Have they already got God's Book in their language?"

"No," replied his father, "but the missionary has visited them many times and some of them, like Raja Lejau, have travelled with him. They remember much of his teaching."

"But the missionary has not visited us again," said Ding, "and now he has gone home. We will never get The Book."

"It is sad that the missionary has gone home," agreed Ding's father, "but Raja Lejau told us not to be discouraged. The missionary has not forgotten us."

"He told us to remember that the Lord Jesus hadn't gone home," added Ding's mother with a smile.

Ding liked that thought. He felt encouraged as he thought about it. However, gloom descended again when he remembered Usun and his unanswered prayer concerning her.

"Did you ask Raja Lejau if he knew why my prayer wasn't answered?" asked Ding.

"No. I did not like to ask him in front of everyone," replied his father. "There was no chance to see him alone. Perhaps we may be able to speak with him when he comes back up-river in a few days."

"Perhaps," answered Ding doubtfully.

That evening as Ding and his friends strolled along the verandah, they talked of the things the Kelabit had told them and voiced their disappointment that the missionary would not be returning.

"Anyi's father is saying that we are foolish to continue following the Jesus Way."

"Yes, and he is talking much about going down to ask that Bungan witchdoctor to come and teach us."

"I wouldn't follow that custom."

"Neither would I, but some of the people are discouraged—especially the older people. They say they don't have the right answers for many of our problems."

"Did you hear that the Kelabit were angry when they heard what had happened to Lihan's baby? They said we should have known that it was wrong to let it die."

"Poor Lihan," thought Ding.

"Anyway," added someone, "I think Anyi's father is planning to go down-river and get that man no matter what anyone thinks."

"Then there will be a lot of persuasive talking and they will keep on about the missionary not coming, and then . . ."

No-one said what would happen but they all felt how easy it would be for the people to turn to the Bungan cult in the face of their disappointment. For the next few days there was much discussion in the long-house, centred around the fact that the missionary had gone home, and there was no-one to teach them. They talked about who 'Bungan' was and what it would mean if they followed such a way of life.

Throughout the discussion it was good to hear many voices praising their present way of life. True the missionary had gone home, but hadn't the Kelabit reminded them that the Lord Jesus hadn't gone home? Weren't their lives much happier and easier since they had started to follow Him?

"When the Kelabit come up-river, we will get them to stay and teach us all they know," suggested Ding's father to many. "They taught us much we didn't know. Let them teach us more. And let us pray that other missionaries will come. There must be more of them in other countries."

It was the night before the witch-doctor was to set off that Widow Bulan became ill. Her illness didn't seem very serious at first, but when Ding and his family came home from the farm the following evening, they were conscious that something was wrong.

A man bathing in the river told them that Widow Bulan was very ill; so ill that she had called for the witch-doctor. This piece of news stunned Ding. Widow Bulan had been so strong and encouraged them all to follow the Jesus way. Now she was calling on the witch-doctor.

Ding and his family went to her room. A big crowd was already gathered. She was a popular old lady, respected and loved throughout the long-house.

She was in her tilung and nobody could see her except those caring for her. The witch-doctor had not yet come.

"Did she really call for the witch-doctor?" asked someone incredulously.

"Yes," said another sadly, "I never thought she would go back to Satan's medicine."

"She has been so strong in following the Jesus Way," said another.

"Easy to be strong when you're well," said one, "but when you're sick and you think you might die, that's different."

"She said she wasn't frightened of death. She said she was going to that place called heaven."

"Yes, but she said that when she was well!"

Across the room Ding saw Anyi and Usun close together. Anyi spoke to Usun. She giggled. Ding felt sick.

Then the witch-doctor arrived. He came in solemn-faced but confident. In his hand he carried the little basket of satanic medicine. A murmur swept the room. Ding looked at his father. His head was bowed. Ding knew he was praying. He wanted to pray too, but looking at Usun reminded him of the unanswered prayer.

There was movement from within the tilung and

Widow Bulan's son came out.

"She wants to be brought out here," he said. "Make space for her."

Somewhat surprised, the crowd moved back. Ding could see that the witch-doctor was pleased. Everyone would be able to see his demonstration of power.

The old lady was brought out and laid on the floor. She indicated that she wanted to sit up. Her son got a small stool, sat on it and supported her in a half-sitting position. The witch-doctor came and sat next to her with his little basket.

Widow Bulan looked at him for a long moment. Then she said slowly and distinctly, "You are a fool, Juk Anyi."

The people were electrified. The witch-doctor was visibly taken aback, both by what she said and by the use of his name. No-one had used his real name for years. It had been changed to 'Baya' (crocodile) in his late teens. He had been very ill so his parents had given him a new name to fool the evil spirits. He had received the title of 'Akem' when his second son had died.

"Throw that rubbish away," said Widow Bulan weakly, pointing with her chin at the satanic medicine. She wasn't wasting words. "Power. You always wanted power," she whispered. No-one made a sound for they did not want to miss a word.

"What has it done for you?" She paused. "You are an evil man." Her eyes went slowly around the room. "Don't be fools," she said. "We have never been better off. This Lord Jesus, He is the true One. Do not let this evil man lead you back into darkness."

The witch-doctor had his head bowed. Ding could hear his knuckle joints cracking in rapid succession.

"Come to your senses, Juk," said Widow Bulan in a softer voice. "Jesus can change even your heart."

"They used to be fond of one another," whispered someone near Ding. "They married, but her mother had a dream and they had to separate. They were each forced to marry someone else."

Widow Bulan closed her eyes. "She's dead," thought Ding. But she opened them again suddenly. She seemed to be straining to see something above their heads.

' Lord Jesus!" she exclaimed, and sank back into her son's arms. She was gone.

Silence reigned for some moments. No-one wanted to speak. Sounds of sobbing gradually broke the stillness. The witch-doctor suddenly snatched up his basket and fled.

29

It was two days after the funeral of Widow Bulan. Her death was still the main topic of conversation. One thing was clear. Most people were adamant that they didn't want a visit from the 'Bungan' witch-doctor.

No-one knew what the witch-doctor was thinking, but they noted that the canoe he had been mending was once more stored under the long-house.

As Ding and some of his friends were bathing in the river that evening, they heard a shout. Looking up they saw the two canoe-loads of Kelabit coming up the river. They poled vigorously to the bank where the boys were bathing.

"When did you come?" Ding asked politely.

"Now we are come," they answered, in typical Kelabit style.

"Where did you come from?"

"We came from Long Akah."

"Was all well down river?"

"All was well."

After this polite interchange the Kelabit started bathing before going up to the long-house. They were night stopping. Ding and his friends finished their bathing and returned to the long-house.

Ding told his father that the Kelabit had arrived. "I will see if I can talk to Raja Lejau," said his father and went out onto the long-house verandah. He did not return for the evening meal. This was not unusual. Often the men became absorbed in conversation and talked until late.

Ding called into Lihan's room on the way to the centre of the long-house. Urei and a friend followed at a little distance. As Ding and Lihan settled themselves down they heard the chief say: "Our Kelabit friends have news for us—good news." He paused; everyone was all attention. "They went to Long Akah," the chief continued unnecessarily. "There they found a letter waiting." He held the letter up for everyone to see. "The news in this letter is good news," repeated the chief. Ding wished he would get on with the news. "This letter is from the missionary." There was a stirring and whispering at that piece of information. "Our brother Raja Lejau, who is able to read these strange markings of the Malay language, tells me it was written five moons ago."

"About the time the missionary went home," thought Ding.

"The missionary regrets that because of ill health he will not be able to come again." He paused. "So the missionary has tried to let us know." Ding felt happier already.

"He said that there will be two missionaries coming to live here after harvest to replace him." There was a gasp all round.

Ding and Lihan looked happily at one another. This was surely the best news they'd had for a long time. After harvest! The letter had been written five moons ago. The new missionaries would surely be here soon.

The chief coughed, and everyone fell silent again. "These two missionaries are women," he informed them.

"Women?" a loud cry this time.

"Haven't they any more men in the missionaries' country?"

"Have these women no husbands?" exclaimed a man near the chief.

The chief considered the question for a moment. "I don't think so; the letter does not mention husbands."

"Surely they would not leave their husbands?"

"Perhaps they are not yet married."

"If they are not married they must be mere girls."

"Perhaps they are looking for husbands?"

"Could mere girls teach us the things we want to know?"

There was another loud cough. Everyone looked at Raja Lejau. "Father," he said to the chief, "may I say a few words?"

"Speak," said the chief. "You are familiar with the ways of the Europeans."

"My father, my brethren, my children," said Raja Lejau politely. "Do not be unduly disappointed. It is true that women are not clever like we men. However these European women are clever about some things. One of them, the letter tells us, is able to make those marks which will make God's Book talk to you in your own language. The other is clever with medicine and will help your sick and teach you many things of wisdom."

He paused. "In their country they do not marry as young as our womenfolk. Some do not marry at all. I am not sure why. Perhaps they are too busy doing this work."

This information caused a hum of voices as everyone discussed it.

"These women will teach you much about the Jesus Way. Do not despise them because they are women."

"We must give them land to make their rice farm," said the chief.

"Who will help them cut down the trees and do the heavy work?" asked someone. "We must help them."

"Who will get their wood for their fires?"

"Or their jungle vine and leaves for making their hats and mats and mending their baskets?"

"We must consider how we can help them in these things."

"Wait." The Kelabit coughed loudly.

"These women are clever, as I said, about some things." He paused. "About other things they know very little. They do not know how to plant rice, make baskets or mats, and to see them light a fire . . ." he laughed heartily. "Not only the womenfolk but some of the men do not know how to make a fire!"

A fresh murmur of voices arose. Strange indeed these Europeans.

Raja Lejau was serious again. "These white people are different," he said, "be kind to them and tolerant of their strange ways. They are good people and they will try to learn our customs. You must help them. One thing is sure —they will help you to know the Lord Jesus. They will teach you what is in God's Book. They will teach you to read it for yourselves."

There followed much discussion. After the discussion Ding and Lihan rose and left. They were elated. True, they were disappointed that the missionary they knew was not coming back; nevertheless these women would translate the Bible into their own language and teach them about the Lord Jesus. That was good.

They sat in Lihan's room for some time, talking. Uppermost in Ding's mind was whether his father had been able to talk to Raja Lejau about Usun.

After a while he left Lihan's room and returned to his own. His father was already there. Ding sat down beside him.

"You were able to talk to Raja Lejau?" Ding asked his father.

"Yes, I talked with him," replied his father. "He was surprised to hear that the Lord Jesus had not answered our prayer for he said there is no greater power than His. Sometimes," he went on, "it would seem He does not answer when we ask for a sick person to get better. Raja Lejau does not understand why. But the Lord Jesus does answer when we pray against evil."

"Did he tell you what we should do?" asked Ding somewhat impatiently.

"He said that he had noticed that prayer was not answered when people were of two hearts," explained Ding's father. "He asked if we had kept any satanic medicine or charms to protect us from evil spirits."

"Did you tell him we had nothing?"

"I told him that there was not one thing left. We are following the Lord Jesus with one heart." Ding remembered how his father had almost kept a charm back.

"What did he say then?"

"He asked if Usun's family had kept anything back."

Immediately there came to Ding's mind some words Imang had spoken when they were throwing out their charms. "I saw Widow Paya' hide some of her things and then tell the missionary she didn't have any more." Widow Paya' was Usun's grandmother. Was there some connection between this and Ding's unanswered prayer? Ding repeated to his father what Imang had said.

"They are all in the same room," mused his father. "I wonder if Usun's parents kept anything back."

"I wonder," said Ding. "But what would that have to do with the Lord Jesus not breaking the spell?"

"Raja Lejau said that where there are such things Satan has not really been cast out. When you follow the Lord Jesus you cannot be double-minded. Even if Usun does not know that the things are in her room they will have a satanic influence on her."

"What can we do?" asked Ding.

"Raja Lejau is going to stay here for a few days and teach us what he knows. He and I are going to talk to Usun's parents."

The following evening Ding's father and Raja Lejau went to visit Usun's parents. Ding went too, but sat away from the group. At first Usun's parents were indignant that they should be questioned about such things as satanic medicine and charms. However when Raja Lejau pointed out that people who had satanic medicine belonged to Satan, they became concerned. He also reminded them of the effect Satan's power was having on their daughter.

Usun's mother became quite agitated. "It is true, it is true," she said at last. "Not only did my mother keep something back, but I did too." She rose and entered the tilung. When she emerged she held a small basket in which charms were kept.

"This basket of charms was given to me by a very powerful witch-doctor who was visiting here when Usun was born. I thought it would do no harm to keep it," she sniffed. "We didn't know very much about the Lord Jesus and I thought it would do no harm to be on the safe side."

"It has done harm, Mother," said Raja Lejau quietly.

Both Usun's parents looked uncomfortable and agreed that it had done some harm. Widow Paya' said she was an old woman and found changes hard to take. She wished somebody would tell her who this Lord Jesus was and what following him was all about.

During the conversation Usun had been sitting listening intently and Ding wondered how much she was taking in. There was an expression of bewilderment on her face.

"Now," said Raja Lejau, "take all these things you have left and throw them in the river."

Late as it was he took Usun's father down to the river. The older man threw them as far out into the river as he could.

"Now we will pray," said Raja Lejau after they had returned to the room.

It was a simple prayer. He prayed that the Lord Jesus would forgive Usun's parents and grandmother for being of two hearts. He asked that they would be helped to follow with one heart.

He then prayed for Usun. Now that the satanic charms had been removed he asked that the power of the love potion be broken: also that Usun would be clean of all its effects. He thanked the Lord Jesus for being able to break satanic power. He also thanked Him for His love in dying for each one upon the cross.

After the prayer there was a short silence. Usun looked puzzled but the dark confused look was gone. "I am sleepy," she remarked, "I am going to sleep."

As Usun passed Ding she lowered her eyes and gave him a shy smile before disappearing into the tilung.

A quiet peace filled Ding's heart. Suddenly he became aware of a figure standing near one of the doorways. The resin light flickered on Anyi's face as he stood there watching. Their eyes met. Abruptly Anyi turned and hurried through the doorway.

"Yes," Raja Lejau was saying to the older people, "the Lord Jesus is greater than Satan—and He is God."